COMPUTING

A Business History

Lars Nielsen

2012
New Street Communications, LLC
Wickford, RI

newstreetcommunications.com

Digital edition published 2011 by
New Street Communications, LLC
Wickford, Rhode Island
newstreetcommunications.com

Print edition published August 2012

Also Available as an Audiobook

Contents

Preface

"Ready or not, computers are coming to the people. That's good news, maybe the best since psychedelics."
- Stewart Brand, "Spacewar: Fanatic Life and Symbolic Death Among the Computer Bums," fifth anniversary issue of *Rolling Stone*, December 7, 1972

The years since 1946 have seen one of the greatest revolutions in the history of mankind. In less than seven decades, computer technology has advanced from the primitive and cumbersome ENIAC mainframe to the compact and elegant PC, thence to the extensive personal and business use of the Internet, and finally to a point where things digital have become a fundamental part of society's DNA. "Computing is not about computers anymore," writes Nicholas Negroponte of the MIT Media Lab. "It is about living."

During these years, the speed of digital innovation grew in step with its ambition and - no small thing - excellence. It also moved at the speed of Moore's Law (first articulated by Intel co-founder Gordon E. Moore in 1965). According to Moore's Law - which proved to be a quite accurate prediction - the number of transistors that could be placed inexpensively on an integrated circuit would double approximately every two years going forward. This exponential improvement in processing capacity, which only grew more rapid with the adoption of the silicon chip in the 1970s, has provided the vital foundation on which all digital innovation (requiring ever-increasing processing speed and memory capacity) has been based.

Steve Jobs, Bill Gates and most other great innovators of the new digital era had not yet even been born as of 1949, the year *Popular Mechanics* breathlessly and ambitiously predicted: "Computers in the future may weigh no more than 1.5 tons." Coming into the world during the mid-1950s, these future technologists and entrepreneurs grew up during the period of America's greatest historical prosperity - a time of profound excellence in education, and a time of robust corporate growth (in part enabled by, and in part itself enabling the development and broad-based adoption of early business data systems). Indeed the greatest looming corporate success story of the 1950s and 1960s was IBM. Despite Dustin Hoffman's character in *The Graduate* being advised to go into "plastics," most young people coming of age in educated households during the 1960s were actually advised to look toward something quite different: computers.

The revolution was *on*, and no number of nay-sayers could stop it. "I have traveled the length and breadth of this country and talked with the best people, and I can assure you that data processings [sic] is a fad that won't last out the year." So said Prentice-Hall's editor-in-chief for business books in 1957. "But what ... is it good for?" asked an engineer at IBM's Advanced Computing Systems

Division when confronted with the idea of the microchip in 1968. As late as the 1980s, technologist Ken Olsen, cofounder of Digital Equipment Corporation (DEC), was heard to insist: "There is no reason anyone would want a computer in their home."

In the end, the greatest of all digital innovations - the personal computer - evolved from without the corporate culture, rather than within - a product of the Woodstock generation. "So we went to Atari and said, 'Hey, we've got this amazing thing, even built with some of your parts, and what do you think about funding us? Or we'll give it to you. We just want to do it. Pay our salary, we'll come work for you,'" recalls Steve Jobs. "And they said, 'No.' So then we went to Hewlett-Packard, and they said, 'Hey, we don't need you. You haven't got through college yet.'" And so it went.

*

Ultimately, the history of business computing is characterized by great successive creative leaps of [informed] imagination: of thinking outside the veritable box; of intellectual bootstrapping from one paradigm to another, the latter always (or nearly always) an improvement. (It is prudent to remember Woody Allen's famous comment with reference to comedy: "If you're not failing every now and again, it's a sign you're not doing anything very innovative.")

4

"Innovation distinguishes between a leader and a follower," notes Jobs. To this, Bill Gates adds: "Never before, in history, has innovation offered the promise of so much to so many in so short a time." And that innovation is nowhere near over. "The Web as I envisaged it," writes its inventor Tim Berners-Lee, "we have not seen it yet. The future is still so much bigger than the past."

In chronicling the first six and a half decades of the digital revolution, this volume comprises what will be, in the final analysis, but the beginning in a far longer tale than we can today imagine. Shakespeare told us that what is past is but prologue. Here, then, is one man's version of that prologue.

Lars Nielsen, 1 July 2011

Amsterdam, Holland

From Military to Marketplace

*"If you don't want to be replaced by a computer, don't act
like one."*
- Arno Penzias, computer scientist

As shall be seen, research and development by the
military-industrial complex of the United States has played
a major role in various aspects of computer development
throughout the decades. This was never so much the case,
however, as in the creation of the very first major
computer, the ENIAC (Electronic Numerical Integrator
and Computer).

Funded by the U.S. Army in 1943 and developed at a
cost of $500,000 by John Mauchly and J. Presper Eckert at
the University of Pennsylvania's Moore School of Electrical
Engineering, the ENIAC was a cumbersome, massive
machine, but also a technological wonder at the time of its
public debut in 1946.

Consider the heft: 17,468 vacuum tubes, 7,200 crystal
diodes, 1,500 relays, 70,000 resistors, 10,000 capacitors and
around 5 million hand-soldered joints. Taking up 1,800
square feet, the ENIAC weighed more than 27 tons.
(Writing in 2004 for the IEEE *Annals of the History of
Computing*, David Allen Grier, a technology historian at
George Mason University, said the machine was best

described "as a collection of electronic adding machines and other arithmetic units, which were originally controlled by a web of large electrical cables.") Today, UPenn's School of Engineering and Applied Science has on display four of the original 40 panels of the ENIAC.

Input was via IBM card reader, and output via IBM card punch. Once the painstaking job of input was finished, actual computing took place at what seemed at the time like warp-speed. A multiplication of a 10-digit number by a single-digit number took 1400 microseconds (714 per second), a 10- by 10-digit multiplication took 2800 microseconds (357 per second), and so forth. A division or square root problem took approximately 28,600 microseconds (35 per second). These speeds were no less than one thousand times faster than those offered by the previous generation of electro-mechanical calculator machines. This quantum leap in computing power has never since been matched with reference to the introduction of any single new machine.

Incorporating recursive functions and lambda calculus, ENIAC was "Turing complete," meaning that it was governed by a firm set of data-manipulation rules which, followed in sequence, would produce the results for any requested calculation performed on arbitrary data. (The name "Turing complete" came from British mathematician and computer scientist Alan Turing, whose ideas led to its conception.) Notably, the machine could be programmed to perform sequences of what at the time were extremely complex operations, including loops, branches, and subroutines.

"ENIAC was the prototype from which most other modern computers evolved," wrote Martin H. Weik in 1961. "It embodied almost all the components and concepts of today's high-speed, electronic digital computers. Its designers conceived what has now become standard circuitry such as the gate (logical 'and' element), buffer (logical 'or' element) and used a modified Eccles-Jordan flip-flop as a logical, high-speed storage-and-control device. The machine's counters and accumulators, with more sophisticated innovations, were made up of combinations of these basic elements. ... The primary aim of the designers was to achieve speed by making ENIAC as all-electronic as possible. The only mechanical elements in the final product were actually external to the calculator itself."

The first six programmers of ENIAC were female, in large measure because this function was seen as being rudimentary, almost clerical, compared to the engineering side of things. Nothing could have been further from the truth. "These women, being the first to enter this new territory, were the first to encounter the whole question of programming," comments Paul E. Ceruzzi, a computer historian at the Smithsonian Institution. "And they met the challenge." Well versed in mathematics, Kay Antonelli, Jean Bartik, Betty Holberton, Marlyn Meltzer, Frances Spence and Ruth Teitelbaum did groundbreaking work, creating fundamental approaches that would influence all generations of programmers going forward. These women built the first sort routine, developed the first software application and instruction set, and defined the first classes in programming. They were innovators of the first rank, without whom the ENIAC would have been a mere shell: a brain sans a mind.

But, as the *New York Times* has noted: "When the ENIAC was shown off at the University of Pennsylvania in February 1946 ... the attention was all on the men and the machine. The women were not even introduced at the event" even though the demonstration program being run was of their invention. Decades would pass before these ladies received formal recognition for their trailblazing efforts. (The last of the ENIAC's initial programming team, Jean Bartik, died at age 86 in March of 2011.)

The primary developers of the ENIAC had big plans for the future commercial use of computers. Founded in March of 1946 as the Electronic Control Company and incorporated in December 1947 as the Eckert-Mauchly Computer Corporation, J. Presper Eckert's and John Mauchly's firm was in 1950 acquired by Remington Rand. (Remington Rand eventually merged with Sperry Corporation, becoming Sperry Rand, which later [1986] merged with Burroughs to form Unisys.)

Eckert and Mauchly's UNIVAC (Universal Automatic Computer) had been commissioned by the United States Census Bureau in 1948 with an eye toward having the machine ready to play an integral role in the 1950 national census. (The computer was delivered in March of 1951.)

The term "universal" was meant to convey the fact that the machine was designed to handle both scientific and business applications, the latter being described by a new term: *data processing.* To develop the UNIVAC, Eckert and Mauchly hired a number of the engineers who had previously worked on the creation of the ENIAC at the Moore School.

Although soon overtaken in the marketplace by mainframes developed by IBM, the computer Eckert-Mauchly created for the Census Bureau was nothing short of elegant, and a marvel of innovation. (Ceruzzi has called it a "technical masterpiece." To this he adds: "Many design features that later became commonplace first appeared in the UNIVAC: among them were alphanumeric as well as numeric processing, an extensive use of extra bits for checking, magnetic tapes for bulk memory, and circuits called 'buffers' that allowed high-speed transfers between the fast delay line and slow tape storage units.")

The UNIVAC weighed 29,000 pounds, used 5,200 vacuum tubes, consumed 125 kW, and performed approx. 1,905 operations per second running on a 2.25 MHz clock. Of most importance to users was the fact, already noted above, that it was the first computer to use magnetic tape for high-speed storage, obliterating the need for punch-cards.

Concurrent with the early phases of development for the UNIVAC, Eckert-Mauchly started a software department which developed a number of ground-breaking tools, including the world's first compiler, this for the language "Short Code." (A compiler transforms source code written in one programming language into another computer language, often having a binary form known as "object code," itself often required to render a program executable on a given piece of hardware. Note that the FORTRAN [Formula Translating System] team led by John Backus at IBM is generally credited as having introduced the first complete, *commercially-viable* compiler, having done so in 1957.)

Eckert-Mauchly also developed the BINAC (Binary Automatic Computer: basically a smaller version of the ENIAC) for the Northrop Aircraft Corporation. This machine was handed over to Northrop in September of 1949. Evidently for various logistical reasons (either because of inadequate packing for transport on the part of Eckert-Mauchly, or because Northrop engineers insisted on reassembling the computer themselves rather than allow Eckert-Mauchly engineers to do the job), the BINAC never ran well for Northrop and was eventually abandoned by the firm.

In time, a total of 46 UNIVAC machines were commissioned and delivered, with the price going up slowly from $159,000 to $1,500,000. (Eckert and Mauchly were great engineers, but lousy businessmen. Their initial binding quote to the Census Bureau of $159,000 had been egregiously conservative. Eckert-Mauchly drastically under-estimated development costs for the machine. This money had to be made up by more aggressive pricing for subsequent installations.) Although the earliest sales of the computer were to government agencies and the military, the UNIVAC was also adopted commercially by the Metropolitan Life Insurance Company, Pacific Mutual Life Insurance Company, General Electric, U.S. Steel, DuPont, Westinghouse, Sylvania and Consolidated Edison.

The UNIVAC was used to produce the first concordance of the Revised Standard Version of the Bible in 1956. The UNIVAC was also used by CBS to forecast the outcome of the 1952 Presidential election, predicting the landslide victory of Eisenhower over Adlai Stevenson, whom most pollsters believed would be the next president. Insurers used the computer to run statistical data for actuarial purposes, Con Edison for predicting power needs, and other firms for scientific purposes related to their research and development efforts.

Virtually all the firms also used the computer for payroll management, material scheduling, inventory control, billing, and general cost accounting. The last UNIVAC mainframe to remain in operation was finally shut down in 1970. (Note: in 1956 the Sperry Rand Corporation - result of the 1955 merger of Remington Rand and Sperry - released the low-cost UNIVAC File Computer, specifically designed for data handling and nothing else. This failed in the marketplace, which much preferred general purpose data processing machines capable of not only data handling but also a range of other tasks.)

At the time Eckert-Mauchly delivered the first UNIVAC, would-be competitor IBM was still deriving almost all of its income from the firm's traditional core business of commercial calculators and tabulators. The firm did, however, have a competitor for the UNIVAC in advanced stages of development, this to be announced in May of 1952. Based on advances being made by mathematician John von Neumann at Princeton's Institute for Advanced Study, IBM's 701 rivaled the UNIVAC as a stored-program computer - bettering the UNIVAC's approach significantly. (That being said, the two machines were basically capable of identical task-loads.)

Another far less ambitious IBM machine, the 650, was announced in 1953 and began shipping in 1954. IBM manufactured 2000 systems before discontinuing the line in 1962. IBM stopped supporting the 650 in 1969. The 650 was designed specifically for users of existing IBM unit record equipment [electro-mechanical punched card-processing machines, so-called "Calculating Punches," like the IBM 604] who wished to upgrade to computers proper.

But while the 650 provided a bridge from the past, the 701 served as a bridge to the future. The 701's memory device was capable of retrieving all digits of a word simultaneously, rather than one at a time as in the slower process of the UNIVAC. Unlike the UNIVAC, it featured plastic as opposed to magnetic metal tape (much faster starting and stopping), and a unique vacuum-column mechanism which inhibited tearing of the tape. Like the UNIVAC, the 701 was designed for both scientific and business (data processing) use. Nevertheless, IBM insiders considered it primarily a machine that would appeal to the military establishment including not only the United States Department of Defense but also aerospace and other firms servicing military contracts. The popular name for the machine in-house at IBM was "defense calculator."

IBM installed the first 701 at their own offices in Armonk, New York, and another at the Los Alamos Nuclear Weapons Laboratory a few months later. There were eventually 19 installations in all, the bulk of these within the military establishment. This was in measure a self-fulfilling prophecy on the part of IBM executives and marketers, who initially saw commercial use of computers as a threat to their traditional core business of selling calculating machines for office environments.

Unlike Remington Rand's marketing approach with the UNIVAC, IBM did not sell the 701, but instead leased the machine at a rate of $15,000 per month. (Not until 1956, as a result of a consent decree negotiated with federal authorities concerned about antitrust issues, would IBM begin to sell its machines as well as lease them. Nevertheless, leasing was always to remain the firm's preferred business model.)

IBM announced another machine, Model 702, in September of 1953 - and delivered the first of these three years later. IBM positioned the 702 both technically and applications-wise as a direct competitor to the UNIVAC. Like the latter, it used magnetic tape, and the binary coding of decimal digits. But it also adopted the 701's basic model for electronic circuits. Like the UNIVAC, the IBM 702 used the Williams Tube (officially the Williams-

Kilburn Tube, named after inventors Freddie Williams and Tom Kilburn): a cathode ray tube developed in 1946 to store binary data, and the first random-access digital storage device.

IBM wound up building only fourteen of Model 702, even though there was great demand from a range of customers. This decision on the part of IBM seems to have been derived from the fact that it had new and better machines on the drawing-board. A decision was made at the board-level that customers (not to mention IBM's profit picture) would be better-served by holding off significant adoptions till the results of IBM's intensive, ongoing R&D could be brought to the street.

The fruits of these R&D efforts were revealed in 1954 with release of the IBM 704, the first commercially-produced computer to incorporate floating point arithmetic. (Note: The programming language LISP was first developed for the 704, as was Max Mathews' MUSIC, the first computer music program.)

Not at all compatible with its predecessor machines, the 704 served up a quantum change in terms of architecture as well as implementations and software. Changes included core memory (replacing Williams Tubes), the addition of three index registers, and an expanded 36-bit word instruction set. The 704 instruction set was to live long as the basis for the entire 700/7000 series of computers. From both a technical and performance point of view, the 704 outdid even a souped-up version of the UNIVAC that would be released in 1956.

Several further improvements were made with IBM 709, released in 1958, for which IBM developed the FORTRAN programming language.

IBM's 700 Series and Remington Rand's UNIVAC shared the top echelon of the mainframe marketplace with another contender, the 1101 ("13" in binary notation) developed by Engineering Research Associates (ERA) and subsequently marketed by Remington Rand after that firm's acquisition of ERA in 1952.

Founded by Howard Engstrom and William Norris, ERA had emerged from a group of cryptographic mathematicians involved with code-breaking for the U.S. Navy during World War II. The man that would turn out to be the firm's most noted employee, however, was not a veteran of the World War II effort but rather a 1951 graduate of the University of Minnesota. Seymour R. Cray was to leave large tracks in the development of digital technology and eventually be dubbed "the father of supercomputing." As Joel Birnbaum, one-time Chief Technology Officer of Hewlett Packard has remarked: "It seems impossible to exaggerate the effect [Cray] had on the industry; many of the things that high performance computers now do routinely were at the farthest edge of credibility when Seymour envisioned them."

Originally developed on commission from the U.S. Navy, the 1101 was designed specifically for scientific and engineering purposes rather than business data processing. As Ceruzzi notes: "The 1103 used binary arithmetic, a 36-bit word length, and operated on all the bits of a word at a time. Primary memory of 1,024 words was supplied by Williams tubes, with an ERA-designed magnetic drum, and four magnetic tape units for secondary storage."

After its purchase of ERA, Remington Rand was therefore able to simultaneously offer two distinct machines: the 1101 (soon supplanted by an improved model 1103, released 1953) for dedicated science and engineering purposes, and the UNIVAC with an emphasis on business processing. In the end, Remington Rand sold a total of 20 installations of the 1101 and 1103, most of these going to DOD agencies and aerospace firms contracting with the government.

Several other corporations joined IBM and Remington Rand in the mainframe marketplace, none with great results.

The Minneapolis-based controls-maker Honeywell, after acquiring the fledgling and as-yet unsuccessful computer division of Raytheon in 1955, delivered a mainframe called the Datamatic 1000 in 1957. The machine was a disaster. Although it worked efficiently, it ran on technology that was already well on the way to being obsolete. Most notably, it used vacuum tubes instead of transistors. Not until the mid-1960s, and the launch of its 200 Series of mainframes, would Honeywell produce a machine in step with current technology, albeit futilely in step, as shall be shown.

General Electric - in 1955 a $3 billion firm and thus a behemoth compared to IBM ($461 million) and Remington Rand ($225 million before its merger with Sperry) - could have had a great shot at seizing a large part of the mainframe marketplace, had corporate management been willing. They were not.

GE developed a very efficient and elegant machine, the OARAC (Office of Air Research Automatic Calculator), for the Air Force in 1953. Although this machine was completely capable of the range of the data processing tasks serviced by the UNIVAC and IBM 700 series, the management of GE decided against marketing the mainframe to private industry. The reasons for this are unclear and much debated, although conventional wisdom suggests that GE valued IBM greatly as a high-volume customer for various GE technologies and preferred to remain IBM's supplier rather than its competitor.

During the late 1950s, GE developed a transistorized computer called ERMA (Electronic Method of Accounting) for automated check-clearing in banks. The project was contracted by the Bank of America and orchestrated by GE engineers in concert with talent from the Stanford Research Institute. The machine proved popular, but it was GE's sole success, given the fact that corporate support for computer R&D remained nil. GE would formally exit the mainframe marketplace in 1970, selling its technology - such as it was - to Honeywell for approx. $200 million.

RCA's foray into mainframes proved to be another *Titanic*-like voyage. Smaller than GE but significantly larger than both IBM and Remington Rand, RCA had - as one might expect - been involved supplying storage tubes for the early machines of other companies. In 1955, they introduced their own machine. The BIZMAC mainframe, as its name implied, was intended for business data processing. But like Honeywell's Datamatic, which would be released two years later, the BIZMAC was out of date before its launch, using inefficient and expensive vacuum tubes as opposed to cheaper and faster transistors. Later on, RCA offered up a line of transistorized computers, the 301 and 501, which met with some (though not great) success. RCA would never be a serious player.

The National Cash Register Company (NCR) and the Burroughs Corporation both unsuccessfully experimented with the development and marketing of mainframes during the 1950s. Eventually Burroughs (which helped pioneer transistorized machines) would emerge in the 1960s as a viable competitor in the field.

During the early 1950s, Philco developed a high-performance transistor called "surface barrier," which it subsequently used in several computers of its own design and manufacture. Philco's SOLO, developed in top secrecy during the mid 1950s under contract to the National Security Agency (NSA), was a robust, fully-transistorized general purpose machine. The firm offered a non-classified model for commercial purposes in 1958. Philco's non-classified TRANSAC S-1000 was soon followed by a slightly improved model: the S-2000. First deliveries were made in early 1960. Although the machine performed reasonably well, Philco sales efforts underperformed compared to those of IBM and Remington Rand, and Philco would never be a significant force in the market.

The Sixties - Hardware

"I think there is a world market for maybe five computers."
- Thomas J. Watson Sr., chairman of IBM, 1943

The son, Thomas Watson Jr. - who became president of the firm in 1952 - was to prove the father quite wrong. As TIME Magazine would comment in 1998: "[Watson Jr.] boldly took IBM - and the world - into the computer age, and in the process developed a company whose awesome sales and service savvy and dark-suited culture stood for everything good and bad about corporate America. No wonder the Justice Department sought (unsuccessfully) to break it up."

In sum, the 1960s would be the decade of IBM, which controlled approx. 70% of the mainframe market by 1960 and would continue to do so throughout the decade. Sales of the market-leading 709 pushed IBM to this dramatic market-share.

Although sometimes not at the very forefront of technological R&D, IBM came to excel at perfecting and integrating new innovations pioneered by others while at the same time minimizing production costs through carefully refined manufacturing parameters. The firm as well offered consistently economical pricing and provided unparalleled product and customer support which became legend throughout the western business world. (In time, the expression "Nobody ever got fired for adopting IBM equipment" would become a common phrase in conference rooms from Tokyo to Hamburg.)

The corporate culture at IBM was nothing if not unique. "Watson [Jr.] promoted 'scratchy, harsh' individuals and pressured them to think ahead," commented TIME. "When IBM engineers complained that transistors were unreliable, Watson handed out transistor radios and challenged the critics to wear them out. He never backed away from conflict [and] he installed a 'contention' system that encouraged IBM managers to challenge one another. Watson was paternal with rank-and-file employees, but he was murder on his lieutenants, in accordance with his dictum that 'the higher the monkey climbs, the more he shows his ass.'"

One major innovation which led to IBM's market dominance was its 1956 introduction of a spinning disk technology for handling random-access storage. Through this technology, IBM provided direct, interactive access to large amounts of data - a key to the further market adoption of mainframes in general. Developed by IBM engineers in San Jose, California, IBM's Model 305 Disk Storage unit used a micro-slice of air as a cushion between the disk and the computer head, thus allowing for rapid rotation. Fifty 24-inch aluminum disks rotating at 1200 rpm provided the attached IBM 650 mainframes with a RAM storage capacity of five million characters.

One of the first adopters of the 305 (soon renamed RAMAC, Random Access Memory Accounting Machine) was United Airlines, which used the technology for its reservations system. RAMAC proved a huge hit when savvy IBM publicists installed a unit in the U.S. Pavilion at the Brussels World's Fair (1958).

Even more important, however, was IBM's introduction in 1959 of the 7090, the transistorized direct descendant of the 709. The 7090 sold for approx. $2,900,000 and was available on a lease for $63,500 a month (half the rental price of a 709). The 7090 was six times faster than the 709, featured a 36-bit word length, and delivered 32,768 words of core memory. In this IBM set a trend for almost all computer technology going forward. While the technology grew to be more and more powerful and efficient, it at the same time descended in price.

Per IBM's sales literature for the 7090: "The six-fold increase in the 7090's speed results largely from the use of more than 50,000 transistors plus extremely fast magnetic core storage. The new system can simultaneously read and write electronically at the rate of 3,000,000 bits of information a second, when eight data channels are in use. In 2.18 millionths of a second, it can locate and make ready for use any of 32,768 data or instruction numbers (each of 10 digits) in the magnetic core storage. The 7090 can perform any of the following operations in one second: 229,000 additions or subtractions, 39,500 multiplications, or 32,700 divisions."

The 7090 could use many programs already developed for the 709 as well as hundreds of programs developed for the old 704. In addition, the 7090's input-output media were compatible with those of all IBM data processing systems. Personnel familiar with the 709 required no formal retraining to gain a technical knowledge of the 7090. In other words, firms could upgrade with ease.

The next upgrade of the machine, the 7094 (introduced in 1962) featured four additional registers. The machine leased for approx. $30,000 per month, and could be purchased for $1.6 million. (In 1981, the first IBM Personal Computer, priced at $1,565, offered up to 256 Kilobytes of core memory, far in excess of the core memory in the 7090, which translated to approx. 150 kilobytes.)

The 7090 and 7094 provided great speed: approx. fifty thousand to 100 thousand floating operations per second. Perfectly capable of advanced scientific and engineering tasks, these machines were as well completely efficient in the range of standard business functions. As stated in an IBM press-release from 1960: "The IBM 7090 will process such large-scale business applications as inventory control, production control, forecasting and general accounting. The 7090 is well-suited for IBM Tele-processing, which in its most advanced form uses a powerful computer as the data processing center of a network of decentralized plant and office input stations. An example is SABRE, an automatic, centralized electronic airlines reservations system developed by IBM for American Airlines. SABRE has two 7090s as its computing nerve center. Another IBM

7090 is solving problems for various customer companies at the IBM Datacenter in the Time-Life Building, New York City."

On the scientific and engineering front, four 7090 systems were incorporated in the Air Force's Ballistic Missile Warning System. Two more 7090 systems were used by Dr. Werner Von Braun's development group at NASA's George C. Marshall Space Flight Center as they worked to develop the Saturn rocket. Von Braun used the machines to simulate Saturn flights, to create the most accurate and detailed trajectory simulations ever plotted, to simulate the real-space effects of design modifications, and to analyze vibration and heat transfer effects caused by interaction of the eight powerful rocket engines in the Saturn booster.

IBM would sell and support the 7000 series to the end of the 1960s, withdrawing the 7094 from the market in July of 1969.

Concurrent with the introduction of the 7090, IBM in 1959 made available the 1401, designed to handle the more limited business computing needs (and budgets) of smaller firms. (Meanwhile, IBM's equally inexpensive 1620 provided an economical solution for those interested in running scientific applications.)

Ideal for payroll and the range of accounting and inventory management applications, the 1401 proved popular. As IBM literature stated: "The all-transistorized IBM 1401 Data Processing System places the features found in electronic data processing systems at the disposal of smaller businesses, previously limited to the use of conventional punched card equipment. These features include: high speed card punching and reading, magnetic tape input and output, high speed printing, stored program, and arithmetic and logical ability. ... New simplified programming techniques make the 1401 extremely powerful and more efficient than many other systems of comparable or even larger size. Variable length data and program instruction words provide maximum utilization of the magnetic core storage; there is no waste of storage capacity as with fixed record length systems. Program steps may be skipped or reread in any desired sequence, a feature which greatly increases programming flexibility."

More than 10,000 of these machines were eventually installed, thus confirming for IBM - and the industry as a whole - the growing voracious demand for robust data processing capabilities not only in government and *Fortune 500* firms, but throughout the business world. IBM marketed the 1401 until 1971.

The 1401's prime competitor was Honeywell's H200. Up to two or three times faster than the 1401, the H200 was capable of executing 1401 programs without recompilation or reassembly. After enjoying a short spurt of success during which several hundred machines were sold, the H200 sputtered when IBM countered with a marketing emphasis on their System/360.

The IBM System/360 - a mainframe computer system family announced in April of 1964 - was a milestone in the industry, and in the history of computing generally. IBM created these machines to handle the complete range of applications, small or large, commercial or scientific. The hardware architecture of the 360 drew a distinct boundary between architecture and implementation, thus allowing IBM to release a suite of compatible designs at different prices. The 360s proved extremely successful in the marketplace, where customers were pleased to purchase a smaller system with the knowledge they would always be able to migrate upward if their needs grew, without having to reprogram application software. The design of the 360 is considered by many to be one of the most elegant ever conceived.

Thomas Watson Jr. was the key promoter of the product. "With IBM clearly on top in the early '60s, Watson took one of the biggest gambles in corporate history," reports TIME. "He proposed spending more than $5 billion - about three times IBM's revenues at the time - to develop a new line of computers that would make the company's existing machines obsolete. The goal was to replace specialized units with a family of compatible computers that could fill every data-processing need. Customers could start with small computers and move up as their demands increased." Of particular appeal was the envisioned computer's ability to "emulate" - a new term as applied in the field - variously the IBM 7070 and 1401. Thus customers migrating to the smaller machine could take their old software along with them.

According to TIME: "This flexibility inspired the name System/360, after the 360 degrees in a circle. The strategy nearly failed when software problems created delivery delays. Panic raced through IBM's top echelons as rivals closed in. A desperate Watson ousted his younger brother Dick as head of engineering and manufacturing for the System/360 project, derailing the younger man's career and filling Watson with shame."

But out of this rubble there blossomed genius. "Few products in American history have had the massive impact of the IBM System/360-on technology, on the way the world works or on the organization that created them," writes IBM architect Steve Will. "Jim Collins, author of *Good to Great*, ranks the S/360 as one of the all-time top three business accomplishments, along with Ford's Model T and Boeing's first jetliner, the 707. It set IBM on a path to dominate the computer industry for the following 20 years. Most significantly, the S/360 ushered in an era of computer compatibility - for the first time, allowing machines across a product line to work with each other. In fact, it marked a turning point in the emerging field of information science and the understanding of complex systems. After the S/360, we no longer talked about automating particular tasks with 'computers.' Now, we talked about managing complex processes through 'computer systems.'" After a staggeringly successful run, IBM discontinued the 360 in 1978. (A heart attack forced Watson to retire at age 57 in 1971. He died in 1993.)

In addition to resulting in a great machine, the 360 project also resulted in a great book, *The Mythical Man-Month* by Fred Brooks - the man who ultimately managed the final development of both the 360 itself and the OS/360 software support package. First published in 1975, this volume is considered a classic in systems development literature. (Note: In addition to *The Mythical Man-Month*, Brooks is also known for his seminal paper "No Silver Bullet: Essence and Accidents of Software Engineering.")

It was in *The Mythical Man-Month* that Brooks first enunciated, and proved, what has since become known as Brooks' Law: "Adding manpower to a late software project makes it later." Although virtually every systems architect and programmer has been introduced to Brooks' Law at one point or another, not all adhere to it - especially in the frantic panic of a chronically late and expensive software project. Some have called Brooks' book "the Bible of software engineering." Brooks in turn has quipped that the comparison comes from the fact that "everybody quotes it, some people read it, and [only] a few people go by it."

Ultimately, Brooks saw programming as a blend of the practical and the mystical: "The programmer, like the poet, works only slightly removed from pure thought-stuff. He builds castles in the air, from air, creating by exertion of the imagination ... Yet the program construct, unlike the poet's words, is real in the sense that it moves and works, producing visible outputs separate from the construct itself ... The magic of myth and legend has come true in our time. One types the correct incantation on a keyboard, and a display screen comes to life, showing things that never were nor could be."

*

By the early 1960s, such organizations as the Internal Revenue Service, Blue Cross, and NASA were deep into the use of IBM equipment, although the latter also used mainframes from Honeywell, Digital Equipment Corporation, and other players. (Note: It was not until 1959 that the United States Department of the Treasury authorized the IRS to completely computerize its functions.)

Early competitors to the 360 gained little traction, and little market share. Popular at weapons laboratories such as Lawrence Livermore, however, was the Control Data Corporation's super-fast 6600, designed by Seymour Cray in 1964 and soon considered the leader of a new class of machines: "supercomputers." But Cray's machine had a major flaw. It was largely incompatible with other machines. Thus most installations adopting the 6600 also wound up adopting a System/360 right along with it.

Another would-be competitor for the 360 was RCA's 501 and 301 machines. Although incorporating one of the first COBOL (Common Business Oriented Language) compilers, these machines were quite slow, and thus offered no serious threat to IBM. In 1964, RCA launched the Spectra 70 series - four machines (two of them using integrated circuits) designed for the express purpose of emulating IBM's 360, but selling at around 40% less. The Spectra 70 machines made significant inroads, but collapsed in appeal once IBM launched its competitively-priced System/370 in 1970.

At the same time that mainframes gained ground, machines dubbed "minicomputers" also began to build a base - not as competition for mainframes, but as adjuncts to the larger systems. These small third generation computers became possible with the rise of ever-more sophisticated integrated circuit and core memory technologies.

Compared to mainframes, which took up the size of a large room, minicomputers were merely the size of a large refrigerator. The first commercially successful mini was DEC's 12-bit PDP-8, released in 1965, of which the firm would eventually sell more than 50,000 units. The PDP had a base cost of $16,000. (Interestingly, DEC's first customer for the PDP in its earliest form - the PDP-1, released 1964 - was the Cambridge, Massachusetts consulting company Bolt Beranek & Newman [BBN], which would eventually become renowned for its role in helping to create the Internet.) Minicomputers (sometimes called "midrange computers") offered relatively high processing power and capacity that matched the needs of mid range organizations.

The developer of the PDP, Digital Equipment Corporation, had been founded in 1957 by Kenneth H. Olsen and Harlan Anderson. A Massachusetts (Route 128) company with close ties to the Massachusetts Institute of Technology, DEC fostered a culture which encouraged Spartan efficiency, loose management and individual innovation. In Digital's management structure, Olsen was the supreme figure who hired smart people and then turned them loose on projects. Olsen gave his engineers responsibility and expected them "to perform as adults," says Edgar Schein, who once taught organizational behavior at MIT and frequently consulted with Olsen over the course of 25 years. "Lo and behold," reports Schein, "they performed magnificently." Gordon Bell, an early DEC employee intimately involved in DEC's greatest successes (later a principal researcher at Microsoft) has commented that all DEC alumni "think of Digital fondly and remember it as a great place to work."

Beginning in the mid 1960s, DEC was destined to grow quickly, due in large measure to the sales of its minis. The firm had revenue of a meager $15 million in 1965, and 876 employees. By 1970, however, revenues were $135 million and the firm's employees numbered 5,800. Even at that size, DEC still boasted nowhere near the corporate heft of IBM. (IBM's 1963 revenue equaled $1.2 billion. 1965 revenue was over $3 billion; and 1970 saw the firm at $7.5 billion.) Nevertheless the smaller firm was selling as many PDP-8 machines as IBM was its 360s. (Note: Another firm growing due to sales of minis was Control Data.)

In 1986, *Fortune* was to describe Ken Olsen as "arguably the most successful entrepreneur in the history of American business." DEC, said the magazine, "changed the way people use computers" and was "IBM's most serious challenger." Indeed, Olsen and Anderson always saw their firm as not just a maker of devices purely ancillary to the mainframe, but also as a mainframe provider. Released at the same time as the PDP-8, DEC's 36-bit PDP-6 (improved in 1966 as the PDP-10) did not put a sizable dent into the market for IBM's 7090 and 360 machines; however, the DEC machine did develop a cult-like following of dedicated users (a following in spirit not unlike those who twenty years later would become dedicated to the Apple Macintosh amid a sea of PCs).

Speaking in 2006, Bill Gates called Olsen "one of the true pioneers of computing," adding "he was also a major influence on my life." Gates traces his interest in software to his first use of a DEC computer as a 13-year-old. It is also worth noting that Gates and Microsoft's other founder, Paul Allen, created their first personal computer software on a DEC PDP-10. "Ken Olsen is the father of the second generation of computing," comments George Colony, chief executive of Forrester Research, "and that makes him one of the major figures in the history of this business." (Note: DEC was acquired by Compaq in 1998, which in turn was acquired by Hewlett-Packard in 2001. The brand no longer endures.)

Despite its religiously-devoted base of users, the PDP-10 posed little threat to IBM. By 1970, IBM had installed no less than 35,000 mainframes across the United States and around the world. As the 60's wore on, industry watchers began to refer to IBM and its most-commented competitors (Sperry Rand, Control Data, Honeywell, Philco, Burroughs, General Electric and Honeywell - a list for which DEC did not even make the cut) as "Snow White and the Seven Dwarfs." Later on, once General Electric and RCA left the industry (GE's computing division being sold to Honeywell in 1970, and RCA's to UNIVAC in 1971), the remaining IBM competitors were most often referred to simply as the "BUNCH." DEC would not finally rank inclusion in the BUNCH until the late 1970s, which saw the release of its successful VAX series of mainframes.

As the 1960s wore on, a profitable ancillary business sprang up in the form of leasing companies: firms buying mainframes (primarily IBM machines) and then leasing them to corporations.

IBM's leasing rates were based on an assumption of a five-year obsolescence schedule. Thus IBM priced leases in such a way as to make back development and manufacturing costs, plus make a profit, within that time frame. The independent leasing firms based their business model upon an assumption that many customers would not necessarily choose to automatically upgrade to next generation IBM machines as soon as these were available, and that therefore mainframes purchased by the leasing firms would have a far larger window within which to pay for themselves. Given this assumption, the leasing firms were at liberty to charge significantly less rent on mainframes than did IBM.

IBM's 1956 consent decree agreement with the Federal government had opened the window for this activity when it forced IBM to began selling as well as leasing its units; but it was not until the 1960s that the third-party leasing business really took off, starting with the 1961 launch of a Brooklyn firm called Leasco.

35

The Sixties - Programming and Systems Engineering

"Computers are useless. They can only give you answers."
- Pablo Picasso, artist

Along with advances in hardware, the sixties also saw steady progress in the creation and use of software programming languages, operating systems and systems engineering paradigms.

Most importantly, the innovation of this period defined the *lingua franca* for all computer languages to come.

1968 saw publication of *The Art of Computer Programming: Fundamental Algorithms* by Stanford computer scientist Donald Knuth, the first in a projected seven volume series. (Since that time, Knuth has been dubbed the "father" of the analysis of algorithms as an art and science.) In this seminal book, Knuth sought to formalize skills and best practices of computer programming which had heretofore been, in his word, mere "folklore" passed on by word of mouth (and imitation) among pioneer practitioners. Knuth showed the theoretical basis for these practices and procedures, and set forward a rubric of understanding upon which programmers working in any machine environment, using any language, could base their work. Previously, programming practices had tended to be machine-specific. Knuth began the process of thinking about programming as a skill based on fundamentals - most of all, fundamental algorithms - which lay at the heart of the functioning of any software running on any machine.

Knuth stressed always that he viewed good programming as ultimately an intuitive art, where elegant code innovated freely, within only the loosest of constraints (think in terms of Jazz), would lead to the best software efficiencies. On the other side of the table sat Edger Dijkstra of the Technical University of Eindhoven in the Netherlands, who in 1968 began thinking and writing about a "structured" approach to programming within a carefully defined and uniform process, which would - he believed, contrary to Knuth - lead to the best result. Increasingly, Knuth's philosophy would reign within the community of pure computer scientists doing research with what seemed, at the time, little business use, while Dijkstra's approach would hold the most sway in programming for practical commercial applications.

That same year of 1968 saw the first ever conference focused on a newly enunciated discipline: software engineering. Sponsored by NATO (then concerned about the veracity and reliability of the software underpinning a range of defense systems), the conference was held in Garmisch, Germany. The idea behind the concept of software engineering was to take randomness out of the process of building software and to create a carefully defined system for programmers to work within. In other words, according to Ceruzzi, to define "the theoretical foundations and disciplines of daily practice that one found in traditional fields of engineering."

Software, it was argued, should be created under rubrics as rigidly defined as those by which civil engineers designed and built bridges, and architects skyscrapers. Likewise, programmers should be officially qualified and certified through special training and testing. Nevertheless, as we shall see, all the best software would inevitably be created by programmers and designers thinking out of the box, adhering only to the most fundamental parameters enunciated by the likes of Knuth. Over time, the formal software engineering process was to result in only the most mundane, all-be-they necessary, application solutions.

Throughout most of the sixties, software (and therefore software development) was largely machine (and provider) specific. For example, IBM developed programs meant explicitly for the 700/7000 series which shipped with the machines as part of IBM's sales/service package. This changed in December 1968 when, in response to antitrust concerns, IBM announced its intention to unbundle its software - in other words, to sell/license software applications separate from hardware sales, rather than forcing the sales of both hardware and software as a unit. The most popular of these applications proved to be IBM's

Customer Information Control System (CICS), which IBM offered as a license at $7,200 per year.

Now, for the first time, there crystallized the idea of "software" as a separate marketable item (and as a sales opportunity ripe for exploitation by organizations not involved in the design and manufacture of hardware). Thus, from the very late 1960s and through the 1970s, third-party mainframe software and systems developers were to play a pivotal role in shaping the business computing environment. Mainframes produced by IBM, especially the 360, held vast potential for applications - in fact far more potential than IBM's in-house programming personnel could effectively exploit. This fact created an enormous opportunity for third-party contractors. Indeed, much of the very best software, systems and implementations for these and other machines would henceforth be developed by outside parties.

In this environment, such firms as American Management Systems (AMS), H. Ross Perot's Electronic Data Systems (EDS), Systems Development Corporation (SDC) and Thompson-Ramo-Woldridge (TRW), not to mention the federally funded SDC and MITRE (both having their roots in the development of the SAGE air defense system in collaboration with the RAND Corporation) rose meteorically in prominence.

Fortuitously, this same time period saw the creation of elegant new programming languages with which software for the new pipeline could be created.

Save for FORTRAN and COBOL - each of which remain in use today after many revisions - most other languages developed as of 1968 had proven failures in the creation of business applications. Conspicuous among these failures was ALGOL (short for Algorithmic Language), pushed by the Burroughs Corporation, which in most people's view was overly complicated in its final iteration. Too lean with its first release in 1960, the language was in turn overly fat in its revised 1968 release. ALGOL-68 provided a vast array of tools which, taken together, were hard to understand and harder still to coordinate. In the end, ALGOL's chief contribution to programming was its inspiration of the far more graceful and tightly structured *Pascal* language, developed by the Swiss Federal Technical Institute's Nicholas Wirth as a response (and solution) to the needless complexity of ALGOL.

Another failure was PL/1 (Programming Language, One) - developed by IBM for its System/360 series. Released in 1964, PL/1 adopted various aspects of COBOL, FORTRAN and ALGOL. However, like ALGOL, it proved to be needlessly complex. More important, perhaps, was the fact that by the time of its release FORTRAN and COBOL had already become staples amongst programmers working on the System/360. Thus few saw the need to adopt PL/1, and the language faded fast.

Elsewhere, the future was brewing. As 1969 inched its way towards the end of the decade, Dennis Ritchie and Ken Thompson, working on a DEC PDP-7 machine at the

Bell Telephone Labs in New Jersey, started to create what would one day be called the UNIX operating system - a multitasking, multi-user computer operating system destined to become highly popular for use in workstation environments. Parallel to this they also built a programming language labeled "B" - a descendant of the old BCPL (Basic Combined Programming Language), a procedural, structured computer programming language designed by Martin Richards of the University of Cambridge in 1966. This would eventually be refined and evolve into the language C, informally defined by Brian Kernighan and Dennis Ritchie in a seminal 1978 book, and thenceforward often referred to as "K&R C." Kernighan's and Ritchie's definition of the language was later, in large measure, to form the ANSI C standard. Both the UNIX operating system and the C language were to exert terrific impacts on software development throughout the 1970s, and beyond, especially with the dawn of object-oriented programming using C/C++.

*

It is important to remind ourselves that while all the above revolutions were happening on the computer landscape, another revolution was happening in the streets. No one needs a tutorial on the rise of the counter-culture during the period of the sixties. That computing and the Woodstock generation came of age at the same point of time would prove fortuitous for both. A freewheeling tendency not to buy into accepted wisdom, and to innovate with abandon, was to typify the best in computing development going forward: the products of free thinkers.

As editor Jim Warren would write in *Dr. Dobb's Journal* - a programming publication founded at the height of the hobbyist movement in the 1970s - the personal computer "had its genetic coding in the 1960s' ... antiestablishment, antiwar, pro-freedom, anti-discipline attitudes."

"The truth is," wrote Theodore Roszak in *From Satori to Silicon Valley*, "if one probes just beneath the surface of the bucolic hippie image, one finds a puzzling infatuation with certain forms of ... technology reaching well back into the early sixties." In the spirit of the inspirational Buckminster Fuller who spoke of "spaceship earth" and sought to write its "operating manual," hippies sought a form of post-industrial, knowledge-based life largely in harmony with the ecosystem. Many found a tool for this in computing.

"Fuller was not alone in extrapolating the technophiliac vision of postindustrial history," writes Roszak. "There were others, each of whom became, at some point, a countercultural favorite. There was Marshall McLuhan, who saw the electronic media as the secret of building a new 'global village' that was somehow cozy, participative, and yet at the same time technologically sophisticated. There was Paolo Soleri, who believed that the solution to the ecological crisis of the modem world was the building of megastructural 'arcologies' - beehive cities in which the urban billions could be compacted into totally artificial environments. And there was Gerard O'Neill, who barnstormed the country whipping up enthusiasm for one of the most ambitious schemes of all: the launching of self-contained space colonies for the millions. For a few years, O'Neill became a special fascination of Stewart Brand, founder of *The Whole Earth Catalog* (later *The Co-Evolution Quarterly*). In each of these cases, one sees the same assumption brought into play: the industrial process, pushed to its limit, generates its own best medicine. Out of the advanced research of the electronics, plastics, chemical, and aerospace industries, there emerge solutions to all our political and environmental problems."

43

Time-Sharing, Third Party Vendors, Antitrust, PLATO, and the Rise of the Integrated Circuit

"People think that computer science is the art of geniuses but the actual reality is the opposite, just many people doing things that build on each other, like a wall of mini stones."
- Donald Knuth, computer programmer

UNIX was largely a product of researchers and engineers at Bell Labs who needed, for their own purposes, a system for computer capacity time-sharing. The concept of time-sharing is simply this: many users in an organization concurrently and interactively (or "conversationally") share the capacity of a single computer resource by means of multiprogramming and multitasking - thus dramatically lowering the cost of computing capability.

By the mid 1960s, MIT had developed an experimental, elementary time-sharing system - the Compatible Time-Sharing System (CTSS) - capable of servicing only three or four users simultaneously. CTTS employed the IBM 7094. At about this same time, the Defense Advances Research Project Agency (DARPA) chose GE computers (specifically the GE-635 and 645 lines of machines) for its own time-sharing experiments.

The popular IBM System/360 lacked dynamic address translation - the capability of stopping program execution, moving it out of core memory and back to disk, and then loading it back to core memory on demand. The GE machines, on the other hand, contained this feature, which was viewed by most engineers as essential for efficient and economical time-sharing. IBM's hasty 1965 introduction of a jury-rigged "Model 67" machine incorporating time-sharing system software (TSS) proved a fiasco, as the randomly engineered machine in no way matched the capabilities of the GE computers. The product failed, and would eventually become infamous in antitrust proceedings as evidence of IBM sometimes launching products not with the idea of enhancing real value for clients, but rather to use its marketing clout to undermine competition. (Eventually, IBM's System/370, popular through the 1970s and 1980s, would incorporate IBM's robust and elegant Conversational Monitoring System [CMS] software for data-intensive time-sharing work.)

But even the GE machines, though far better suited than the 360 or Model 67, were not absolutely optimal. GE wound up killing its time-sharing project, which it had dubbed MULTICS, in 1969. It was in the midst of this that Bell Labs began development of UNIX - a superb simplification of both the CTSS and MULTICS paradigms which, as has already been mentioned, they ran on a DEC PDP-7 and later a PDP-11. Thus, for the near future at least, DEC machines would be closely associated with the UNIX operating system, to the benefit of both.

*

As has already been noted, IBM's 1968 decision to "unbundle" its software was made in response to antitrust pressures from the federal government. It had been the hope of IBM executives that such action, combined with its earlier decision to sell as well as lease its machines, would head off antitrust proceedings against the firm. This proved not to be the case. In mid-January 1969, right at the tail-end of the Johnson administration, the U.S. Justice Department filed an antitrust action against the firm.

The Justice Department charged IBM with violating Section 2 of the Sherman Act by attempting to monopolize the "electronic digital computer system market." Investigations and proceedings related to this action were to continue until 1982 when, as the rise of the PC began to make the mainframe look more and more like a dinosaur, the government would summarily drop the case. Nevertheless, these and other antitrust proceedings were to be a major distraction for IBM throughout the decades going forward.

*

Along with UNIX, other hints - or "seeds," if you will - of the future continued to appear. The most interesting -

and perhaps tragic - of these was the PLATO machine developed by CDC and its visionary president Bill Norris in the mid 1970s. Providing a unique window into what was to come, this system (featuring a graphics-based interface) was designed specifically for education - built with the idea of servicing students from kindergarten on up to professional schools and colleges. Along with the ground-breaking notion of a graphical user interface (GUI), the CDC-mainframe based PLATO was also built around the idea of students having instant, interactive access to information from libraries and archives around the globe. Thus were not only the Macintosh and Windows interfaces presaged by PLATO, but also the World Wide Web. PLATO's technology, however, proved far too expensive to be practical for educational institutions. The promise of its innovations would have to wait for advancing technology to bring costs down across the board.

Another key development was the growing impact of integrated circuits. Back in July of 1958, Jack Kilby of Texas Instruments had jotted some rudimentary ideas concerning the integrated circuit, and he successfully demonstrated the first working example on September 12, 1958. Applying for a patent on February 6, 1959, Kilby (who would win the 2000 Nobel Prize in Physics for his part in the invention of the IC) described his new device as "a body of semiconductor material ... wherein all the components of the electronic circuit are completely integrated." At about this same time, Fairfield Semiconductor's Robert Noyce came up with his own idea of an integrated circuit, but did it better. How? Noyce made his chip of silicon, while Kilby's chip was germanium-based.

The first integrated circuits offering "small scale integration" - SSI - employed only a few transistors (numbering in the tens) on each chip. These were used in the Minuteman Missile and Apollo projects, both of which demanded very lightweight onboard computers for inertial guidance systems. In turn, the late sixties saw "medium scale integration" - MSI - devices which contained hundreds of transistors on each chip. Then, in the mid 1970s, there came "large scale integration" - LSI - tens of thousands of transistors on each chip.

Various integrated circuits (such as 1K-bit RAMs, calculator chips, and the first microprocessors) which began to be manufactured in moderate quantities in the early 1970s, had under 4000 transistors. True LSI circuits, approaching 10000 transistors, began to be produced around 1974 for computer main memories and second-generation microprocessors. Not until the early 1980s would the industry become capable of "very large scale integration" - VLSI. These circuits offered hundreds of thousands of transistors at the time, and today can contain several billion transistors. By 1970, a number of semiconductor companies (not the least INTEL, founded by Robert Noyce, Gordon Moore and Andy Grove) were in line to supply a reliable flow of economically-priced MSIs.

IBM's System/370, launched (as has been noted) in 1970, replaced the 360's solid logic technology circuits with

ICs. However, the rise of the IC influenced the minicomputer marketplace far more than it did the mainframe marketplace, in the latter of which IBM was destined to remain dominant.

Up and coming tech entrepreneurs saw opportunities in the minicomputer marketplace that they did not see in the mainframe universe. Where IBM's domination of mainframes seemed unassailable, DEC's domination in the mini marketplace appeared considerably less so. DEC was not perceived as an overpowering monopoly, a 300-pound gorilla. Per Ceruzzi: "DEC did not dominate in minicomputers in the same way IBM dominated mainframes. ... DEC's competitors did not feel they had to answer every product announcement, or offer software-compatible products. Technical innovation, at low cost and in a compact package, mattered more."

The lowering costs of chips and other aspects of manufacture led to the founding of hundreds of DEC competitors, either as new firms or as subsidiaries of older companies. While venture capitalists were uniformly unwilling to fund ventures designed to compete with the monolith IBM, they were quite open to firms wanting to explore and exploit the growing, open and increasingly-profitable market in minicomputing.

Still, DEC remained a formidable force. The firm's PDP-11 machine, launched in January of 1970, represented a complete rethinking of the traditional PDP architecture. The machine's greatest innovation was a 56-line "Unibus" uniformly connecting just about all the major units (memory, I/O devices) of the machine. This innovation made it relatively simple for customers to configure specialized apps, making the machine easily and inexpensively adaptable for a broad range of purposes. To this day, the bus architecture remains central to all computer design.

Despite meaningful competition, the PDP-11 quickly came to be the System/370 of minicomputers as regards popularity. Throughout the 1970s, DEC sold more than 170,000 units. The firm, which had boasted 5,800 employees in 1970, in turn boasted 36,000 employees by 1977.

It is important to point out yet another mini of this era which, though only marginally successful in the marketplace, proved to be quite groundbreaking from a technical point of view: Data General's Nova/Super Nova line. This machine was the brainchild of engineer Edson DeCastro. When a DEC employee working on the creation of a 16-bit mini which DEC called the PDP-X, DeCastro had his design turned down by DEC executives. Thus, in early 1968, a disgruntled DeCastro and two co-workers departed DEC to found their own firm, Data General.

Their Nova, announced in the autumn of that year, was an elegant example of stripped down yet powerful design. The Nova incorporated features which would revolutionize computer design in coming years. Foreshadowing the silicon revolution, the Nova was the first machine to fully deploy MSI chips. Nova's design called for these chips to be mounted on a single printed circuit board, thus enabling the computer to have a much smaller physical presence than comparative machines. Of equal importance, this machine's descendant, the Super Nova introduced in 1971, was the first to use integrated circuits rather than magnetic cores for RAM. Recent advances in the design and use of semiconductor memory enabled the economical deployment of this mode of RAM, thus making the innovation affordable for commercial machines.

But as shall be shown, some of the most interesting innovations of this period were not happening in corporate labs, but rather in garages and basements across the United States where a scattered subculture of precocious, long-haired kids tinkered with wires and circuit boards and rudimentary I/O devices.

Hobbyists, Microsoft and DOS

"At our computer club, we talked about it being a revolution. Computers were going to belong to everyone, and give us power, and free us from the people who owned computers and all that stuff."
- Steve Wozniak, co-founder of Apple

In April of 1972, Intel announced a chip called the 8008, which could handle data in 8-bit chunks. Two years later, the firm announced the 8080, capable of addressing much more memory while at the same time needing fewer support chips. As would become a trend, the 8080 was configured so as to make programs designed for the 8008 upwardly compatible.

The March 1974 issue of *QST* - catering to amateur builders of radios - carried an ad for a kit to build a small computer called the *Scelbi-8H*. This machine used an 8008 chip and had pricing that started at $440. Two months later the magazine *Radio-Electronics* offered for $5 the plans to build another 8008-based machine: a "personal minicomputer" called the *Mark-8*. These plans included referrals to firms where would-be builders could buy circuit boards ($47.50) and 8008 chips ($120.00). Six months on down the road, in January of 1975, *Popular Electronics* offered the kit for H. Edward Roberts' Altair computer, which could be assembled for just under $400.

Working out of a garage in Albuquerque, New Mexico, Roberts had co-founded Micro Instrumentation and Telemetry Systems (MITS) in 1969. The firm's Altair signaled a real revolution, because the Altair, centered on an Intel 8080 microprocessor, was the real deal: an actual personal computer. Many consider the introduction of the Altair as an event of equivalent importance to IBM's introduction of the System/360 in the previous decade. This machine, per the article in *Popular Electronics*, was "a full-blown computer that can hold its own against sophisticated minicomputers ... not a 'demonstrator' or a souped-up calculator." The Altair offered "[performance that competes] with current commercial minicomputers," the latter being priced, on average, ten times higher than the Altair.

The Altair's computer bus was to become a *de facto* standard in the form of the S-100 bus.

Roberts had expected to sell about two hundred Altair kits, even though he'd given his financial backers an optimistic forecast of 800. Instead he sold thousands.

The introduction of the Altair 8800 happened at just the right moment. For more than ten years, colleges had required students majoring in science and engineering to take at least one course in computer programming. Most of these courses involved either learning FORTRAN or BASIC (the latter being "Beginner's All-purpose Symbolic Instruction Code," originally designed at Dartmouth as a teaching tool). This in turn led to the creation of a sizable informed (and inquisitive) customer base well-prepared to receive the Altair and other similar machines.

The $400 Altair kit allowed one to build a bare-bones, stripped-down machine. But with the simple addition of an expansion chassis, slots became available into which numerous cards could be plugged. MITS designed and sold some cards delivering memory, I/O, etc. Importantly, so did other vendors. As Ceruzzi writes: "Following the tradition established by Digital Equipment Corporation, Roberts did not hold specifications of the bus as a company secret. That allowed others to design and market cards for the Altair. ... So while it was true that for $400 hobbyists got very little, they could get the rest - or design and build the rest. Marketing the computer as a bare-bones kit offered a way for thousands of people to bootstrap their way into the computer age, at a pace that they, not a computer company, could control."

The first programming language for the machine was Altair BASIC - an interpreter scaled especially for the Altair by Harvard students Bill Gates and Monte Davidoff together with Gates' old Seattle friend Paul Allen (at that time a programmer for Honeywell in Boston). The three did their work running an Intel 8080 simulator on a Harvard DEC PDP-10. Per Ceruzzi: the ambitious team "wrote not only a BASIC that fit into very little memory; they wrote a BASIC with lots of features and impressive performance." Most significantly, unlike previous BASIC interpreters, this one provided a USR (user service routine) with which programmers could easily switch from BASIC commands to instructions written in machine language, thus compressing the language so as to make it more useful on small machines. (This exercise, and the interpreter's adoption by Altair, led in turn to the founding of the firm at first called "Micro Soft." Davidoff - who designed the floating point arithmetic aspect of the interpreter - did not join Gates when the latter dropped out of Harvard to start the Micro Soft partnership with Paul Allen. Davidoff did, however, work with Gates at Microsoft over the course of a couple of summers, creating subsequent improved releases of what started as Altair BASIC but eventually became known as Microsoft BASIC.)

Hobbyist clubs and mutual user-support groups quickly sprang up around the Altair. In what would become known as "Silicon Valley" there emerged the "Homebrew Computer Club" (founded March 5, 1975 by Lee Felsenstein, who later designed the first Osborne computer). 25-year-old Hewlett-Packard engineer Steve Wozniak became a regular, attending meetings which at first were held in a Menlo Park garage.

"The people in Homebrew were a mélange of professionals too passionate to leave computing at their jobs, amateurs transfixed by the possibilities of technology, and techno-cultural guerrillas devoted to overthrowing an oppressive society in which government, business, and especially IBM had relegated computers to a despised Priesthood," wrote Steve Levy in *Hackers*. "Lee Felsenstein would call them 'a bunch of escapees, at least temporary escapees from industry, and somehow the bosses weren't watching. And we got together and started doing things that didn't matter because that wasn't what the big guys were doing. But we knew this was our chance to do something the way we thought it should be done.'"

"Our club in the Silicon Valley, the Homebrew Computer Club, was among the first of its kind," Wozniak recalls. "It was in early 1975, and a lot of tech-type people would gather and trade integrated circuits back and forth. You could have called it *Chips and Dips*. We had similar interests and we were there to help other people, but we weren't official and we weren't formal. ... This was before big personal computer firms and big money considerations. There was just one personal computer then, the Altair 8800, based around the Intel 8080 microprocessor." By 1976 the Homebrew Computer Club had 750 members (up from 32 at the first gathering).

Innovation flourished in both hardware and software. Wozniak and other young tech rebels smelled liberation in the air. Theodore Roszak recalls how "in its early days, home computer invention and manufacturing did resemble a sort of primitive cottage industry. The work could be done out of attics and garages with simple means and lots of brains. The people pioneering the enterprise were cut from the mold of the Bucky Fuller maverick: talented drop-outs going their own way and clearly outflanking the lumbering giants of the industry, beating them to the punch with a people's computer ... even before the personal computer had matured into a marketable commodity, there were idealistic young hackers who wanted to rescue the computer from the corporations." In this environment, a share and share-alike mentality pervaded with regard to both knowledge and software.

Not everyone liked that idea. After dropping out of Harvard and going to New Mexico to found his firm, the ambitious young Bill Gates quickly became concerned about the protection of software as intellectual property. In a now famous "Open Letter to Hobbyists" dated February 3, 1976, Gates wrote: "Almost a year ago, Paul Allen and myself, expecting the hobby market to expand, hired Monte Davidoff and developed Altair BASIC. Though the initial work took only two months, the three of us have spent most of the last year documenting, improving and adding features to BASIC. Now we have 4K, 8K, EXTENDED, ROM and DISK BASIC. The value of the computer time we have used exceeds $40,000. The feedback we have gotten from the hundreds of people who say they are using BASIC has all been positive. Two surprising things are apparent, however, 1) Most of these 'users' never bought BASIC (less than 10% of all Altair owners have bought BASIC), and 2) The amount of royalties we have received from sales to hobbyists makes the time spent on Altair BASIC worth less than $2 an hour."

Gates warned that if the practice of pirating software continued it would "prevent good software from being written. Who can afford to do professional work for nothing? What hobbyist can put 3-man years into programming, finding all bugs, documenting his product and distribute it for free? The fact is, no one besides us has invested a lot of money in hobby software. We have written 6800 BASIC, and are writing 8080 APL and 6800 APL, but there is very little incentive to make this software available to hobbyists. Most directly, the thing you do is theft. What about the guys who re-sell Altair BASIC, aren't they making money on hobby software? Yes, but those who have been reported to us may lose in the end. They are the ones who give hobbyists a bad name, and should be kicked out of any club meeting they show up at. I would appreciate letters from anyone who wants to pay up, or has a suggestion or comment. ... Nothing would please me more than being able to hire ten programmers and deluge the hobby market with good software."

Gates' notion ran contradictory to the common philosophy at the time that if one interpreter for a language was free, then all should be, despite any enhancements contained in an individual release. The originators of the BASIC language at Dartmouth had never sought to commercialize it. DEC, which later added many useful extensions, had given its interpreter away for free, as it did all software bundled with the hardware which the firm viewed (correctly) as their profit-center. But, as Ceruzzi notes: "Gates had recognized what [many] had not: that with the advent of cheap, personal computers, software could and should come to the fore as the principal driving agent in computing. And only by charging money for it - even though it had originally been free - could that happen."

Gates' idea that his BASIC and other such products should be viewed as proprietary did not gain quick acceptance. "There is a viable alternative to the problems raised by Bill Gates in his irate letter to computer hobbyists concerning 'ripping off software,'" wrote the unsympathetic Jim Warren of *Dr. Dobb's*. "When software is free, or so inexpensive that it's easier to pay for it than to duplicate it, then it won't be 'stolen.'" (Note: the price for a 4K version of BASIC was $60. An 8K version went for $745, with an additional $150 fee for extended enhancements which required some form of storage attached to the Altair. A version that could run on any non-Altair 8080-based system cost $500.)

Most hobbyists, meanwhile, had other concerns and interests.

Initially, the Altair provided no way to store data. Memory died as soon as the power was shut off. In time, Roberts and his small team at MITS created a way to translate data into audio tones which could be stored on cassettes. Subsequently, during the autumn of 1975, a small coven of Kansas City hobbyists established a standard for computer audio tones - thereby creating a method by which programs became portable from one Altair to another. Very soon, however, floppy disks emerged as the storage hardware of choice.

Somewhat ironically, a strong software operating system for floppies was developed - though not widely distributed - well before others explored the more primitive audio-cassette approach. It was one Gary Kildall

- whom Gates would eventually salute as "one of the original pioneers of the PC revolution" - who created the first microprocessor system software.

While working as a math and computer science instructor at the Naval Postgraduate School in Monterey, Kildall in 1973 developed the first high-level programming language for microprocessors: PL/M. In that same year, he created CP/M (Control Program for Microcomputers), with which he armed the 8080 to control a floppy drive. Thus Kildall combined all the essential components of a computer at the microcomputer scale.

CP/M was not presented to the wide hobbyist public until April of 1976, when Jim Warren wrote an article for *Dr. Dobb's Journal* in which he hailed CP/M as a breakthrough. Shortly before, Kildall and his wife Dorothy had established a company - Digital Research, Inc. (DRI) - to further develop and market CP/M.

DRI licensed CP/M for the IMSAI 8080, a popular clone of the Altair 8800, and to numerous other manufacturers. Within a year or so, CP/M became a *de facto* standard. Kildall's main development focus, meanwhile, became the idea of a BIOS (Basic Input/Output System): a set of rudimentary programs stored in the computer hardware which enabled CP/M to run on different systems without modification. CP/M reached the peak of its popularity in 1981, at which time it ran on 3,000 different computer models and DRI saw $5.4 million in annual revenue.

"After the IMSAI deal," wrote Michael Swaine in *Dr. Dobb's Journal*, "Digital Research began to grow rapidly. Although it wasn't a financial necessity, Gary continued to teach at the Naval Postgraduate School for several years after the founding of DRI. DRI itself felt very academic. Relationships tended to be collegial, the atmosphere casual, discussions animated and cerebral. Or not so cerebral: The atmosphere sometimes was less like a college classroom than a college dorm. Gary liked to roller-skate through the halls, and once conducted an employee interview in a toga."

But competition was out there. And in some measure, DRI's "success" was nothing but a short-term illusion. As shall be discussed in further detail later, 1977 had seen the launch of Apple's premier product, the Apple II, which quickly became a bestseller. "In the early '80s, the Apple II was the largest-selling machine that did not run CP/M, but it was also the largest-selling machine, period," notes Swaine. "The base of software for CP/M systems was large and growing, and Microsoft, seeing an opportunity, [in 1979] made an uncharacteristic move into hardware: it developed a SoftCard for the Apple II that would let it run CP/M. Then it licensed CP/M from DRI to sell with the SoftCard. Soon Microsoft was selling as much CP/M as DRI." And DRI, despite its good numbers, was nevertheless missing out on direct sales to its largest potential market.

1981 saw Kildall make another strategic blunder - a major one. For complex and often-disputed reasons,

Kildall - despite overtures from IBM - failed to license CP/M (in fact, a new version in development, CP/M 86) for use as the exclusive operating system powering IBM's much-anticipated new line of PCs. In the wake of this, IBM asked Bill Gates and his colleagues at what was now called Microsoft - they already being at work on a BASIC interpreter for the forthcoming IBM PC - to either find or build an appropriate operating system. Responding to this request, Paul Allen arranged a licensing deal for a CP/M clone (86-DOS) marketed by Seattle Computer Products (SCP). Microsoft re-engineered this slightly for IBM's hardware, and prepared it to ship as PC-DOS.

Examining PC-DOS before its general release with the IBM PC, Kildall concluded that the operating system infringed on many aspects of his CP/M. After Kildall threatened IBM with legal action, IBM told Kildall they would offer CP/M-86 as an option for the PC in return for a release of liability. Kildall accepted.

Thus, when the IBM PC was first introduced as IBM Model Number 5150 on August 12, 1981, IBM sold its operating system as an unbundled option. For the first few months of PC sales, however, customers had only PC-DOS ($40) from which to choose. Kildall did not get his CP/M-86 out the door until several months later, and then priced it at $240. So ended the life of CP/M; and so began the meteoric rise of Microsoft, now based in Seattle. The episode would lead *Business Week*, looking back in 2004, to call Kildall "the man who could have been Bill Gates."

Kildall eventually sold his company to Novell and became rich. He remained with the firm for a while but, as notes Michael Swaine: "At Novell, all traces of DRI products and projects quickly dissolved and were absorbed like sutures on a healing wound." After leaving Novell, Kildall "did charitable work in the area of pediatric AIDS. It should have been a good life, but all was not sublime. His second marriage was ending in divorce, and there were signs that lack of credit [for his role in the start of the PC revolution] was continuing to eat at him." He died in 1994 at the age of 52.

The Woz and Steve Jobs

"To turn really interesting ideas and fledgling technologies into a company that can continue to innovate for years, it requires a lot of disciplines."
- Steve Jobs, co-founder of Apple

Throughout the 1970s, businesses continued to focus on the use of mainframes and minis for the bulk of their computing tasks, while in the realm of office automation firms like Viatron, Xerox and Wang Labs set about marketing dedicated word-processing systems. Wang, in particular, met with quite a bit of success through its WPS (Wang Word Processing System) launched in June of 1976.

A rudimentary system incorporating hard disk storage went for $30,000. Given the fact that typists at the time worked for an average wage of between $1.25 and $1.50 per hour, the economics of the system generally did not make much sense under the scrutiny of a rigorous cost-benefit analysis. But the romance of the machine took hold, at least for a time. Ultimately, the days of dedicated word processors were to be quite limited - lasting not more than a decade or so before PCs would take offices by storm.

One of the first machines to make this inroad was to be the Apple II, which had its roots in the Homebrew Computer Club.

Steve Wozniak had, for years, fantasized about and conceptualized one small personal computer after another, setting their specs down on paper, and dreaming of the day when chip technology would catch up with his singular vision. Woz had even gone so far as to write FORTRAN compilers and BASIC interpreters for these vaporous machines.

In April of 1974, along came the 8080 chip which, though it made Woz's vision suddenly practical, lay way beyond his budget at $179. Not long after, Woz discovered another chip option - one far more elegant and far more affordable. The operations of the Motorola 6800 resembled those of the Data General Nova minicomputer, which Woz thought particularly efficient. As a bonus, a near-identical clone of the 6800 - MOS Technology's 6502 - sold for just $25.00. (The price for the Motorola chip was equivalent to that of the 8080 at $175.)

Wozniak promptly wrote a BASIC interpreter for the 6502. At the same time, he and a colleague took a Hewlett-Packard mini and programmed it to simulate the function of the 6502. Here, on this machine, Wozniak worked whenever time allowed, and tested his routines. Once the BASIC interpreter was bulletproof, he turned his attention to designing the hardware he could run it on.

In a dramatic innovation, Wozniak enabled his machine with connections for a keyboard (sold separately and to be installed by the user) - a vast improvement over the Altair's sequence of front panel switches. As well, he created connections whereby a television set could easily be connected and made into a rudimentary video terminal. Wozniak used two 256 x 4 PROM (programmable read-only memory) chips to create a 256 byte "monitor" program that served as a simple operating system, automatically booting with the machine.

With a further eye toward economy, Wozniak employed shift registers to relay text to the television screen, thus avoiding the need for expensive RAM chips. This slowed down the video terminal a bit, as the system only allowed for the display of about 60 characters per second.

When armed with a full board, Wozniak's machine featured 8K of dynamic RAM. This allowed for the loading of the BASIC interpreter (approx. 4K) and an equivalent amount of memory for programming. Power was supplied by two transformers providing a total of 17 volts for the motherboard. Also, per one Apple historian: "There was a single peripheral slot, and when it was first released there was nothing available to plug into this slot. It was entirely contained on a single printed circuit board, only sixteen by twelve inches in size (most hobby computers of that time needed at least two boards), used only 30 or 40 chips, and because it could run BASIC programs it got people's attention."

By early 1976, Wozniak had a fully-functioning machine which he'd show-off at Homebrew Computer Club meetings, updating friends regularly with regard to ongoing tweaks and enhancements, and also gathering comments and suggestions.

Enter Steve Jobs. Just a few years younger than Wozniak, Jobs was a good friend with whom Woz had once designed an arcade game - "Breakout" - for the Atari. Jobs hovered over Wozniak's shoulder all during the design of his computer, and made several key suggestions which were incorporated into the final version. Jobs, more the entrepreneur, promoter and salesman as opposed to Wozniak the pure technologist, early on proposed to Wozniak that they manufacture a few printed circuit boards for Wozniak's machine and sell these to those members of the Homebrew Computer Club who might want to build their own computers along Woz's design.

Pooling their meager financial resources and selling the circuit boards as their first product, the two formed Apple Computer Company on April 1 - April Fools' Day - 1976. Jobs had recently worked at an organic apple orchard, and liked the name because - as he told an interviewer years later - apples were healthy, came in an efficient and attractive package, and were in all ways "perfect." In turn Jobs, who never lacked for ambition, wanted the firm to grow into the "perfect" company.

The firm's first logo showed an apple about to drop down onto the head of Sir Isaac Newton, inspiring his great revelation about gravity. Through the years, some writers have suggested that the name was chosen in some sort of homage to the Beatles, whose record label bore the same moniker. This seems not to have been the case, though in the coming decades the potential infringement on the Beatles trademark was to cost Apple serious dollars in licensing fees paid to the Beatles' firm.

Acting as Apple's salesman in chief, the enthusiastic and tirelessly confident Jobs approached Paul Terrell, founder of a computer store (a new concept) in the Bay area: "The Byte Shop." Jobs asked Terrell to stock Apple boards. Terrell told Jobs he was only interested in selling fully assembled machines (just the computer, minus monitor, keyboard and power-supply). He offered to purchase fifty.

Working together with no other assistance, Jobs and Wozniak built the machines - now called Apple-1 - in Jobs' garage using parts they'd bought on credit. Released in July of 1976, the Apple-1 sold for $666.66: approximately twice the cost of the parts plus a 33% dealer markup. Eventually, Jobs and Wozniak assembled a total of two hundred Apple-1 computers, all but twenty-five selling over the course of a ten month period.

Soon, at the request of Terrell, Wozniak designed an interface for a cassette peripheral. The small printed circuit board - which sold for $75 with a cassette of Wozniak's BASIC interpreter thrown in for free - plugged into the one and only expansion slot on the Apple-1 motherboard. On literature packed with the circuit board, Apple opined: "Our philosophy is to provide software for our machines free or at minimal cost." The interface ran fast for its time (1200 baud, when most other cassette interfaces ran at 300 baud). As a further improvement, the Byte Shop arranged for the manufacture of simple koa-wood cases to house the naked circuit board, thus making the package far more attractive.

That same summer, Jobs arranged for Apple's machine to be sold in the the first personal computer store on the eastern seaboard: Manhattan's Computer Mart. Jobs also demonstrated the machine at a meeting of the Association for Computing Machinery, where it generated much excitement. Apple-1 was as well a hit at PC '76 held in Atlantic City, New Jersey on August 28, 1976 - upstaging two other 6502 machines on display. For Jobs, it seemed like the future was there for the taking.

The Personal Computer Comes of Age

"Atari promises to be the most popular Personal Computer System of the 1980s!"
- Atari advertisement, 1980

During the summer of 1977, Radio Shack began marketing the TRS-80 (Model 1) with a price for a basic model starting at approximately $400. The machine's chip, the Z-80, was a bit more powerful than the 8080. The machine came assembled, complete with monitor, keyboard, cassettes, and a start-up routine and BASIC burned into read-only memory (ROM). The machine was practical, efficient and competitive. Sales boomed, being helped along significantly by Radio Shack's staggeringly large storefront footprint across the United States. Also released at about this time was Commodore's moderately priced PET. Commodore's PET used the 6502 chip. Though not dramatically successful in the United States, the PET found a better reception in Europe. Concurrently, the Atari 2600 proved very popular stateside - but solely for game purposes. Atari was never to be able to break out of that niche. None of these items compared favorably with the Apple II, released in April of 1977.

The 8-bit Apple II represented a revolution in design above and beyond what the Apple-1 had offered. Despite being much more highly priced, the Apple II dramatically outsold all of its key competitors. A 4K RAM model sold for $1,298, a 48K RAM model for $2,638. Peripherals were priced separately. The machine's external 143K floppy drive - introduced in 1978 - sold for $495. This included operating system software and a controller which plugged into one of eight internal expansion slots of the bus architecture. The Apple II shipped with Woz's integer BASIC in ROM (later, as of August 1977, with a licensed and better Microsoft BASIC customized for the 6502). Operating system and hardware enhancements would become a regular occurrence throughout the machine's sixteen year production life, eventually moving up to 16-bit capabilities.

Somewhere between five and six million Apple II series computers would be sold by the end of production in 1993.

It did not take long before cool software started to be written for all the popular machines, but most especially for the Apple II.

The most important of these was Dan Bricklin's and Robert Frankston's *VisiCalc* (the first commercial spreadsheet - or visual calculator - application) released in October of 1979. The partnership of these two men was formally known as Software Arts. Bricklin had worked for DEC and was a graduate of the Harvard Business School. Frankston had worked as a programmer on major projects at MIT. Although they at first envisioned their software as a tool to run on DEC machines, Bricklin and Frankston wound up - through the happenstance of availability - doing most of their development on an Apple II.

The end-product was efficient, clean and - for the time - reasonably intuitive. Choosing to focus on hardware, Apple declined to market *VisiCalc*, which Software Arts priced at about $200. Despite the lack of Apple's direct support, *VisiCalc* took off immediately. Suddenly, business users - especially those from small businesses, which heretofore had not been able to afford robust financial processing software - became very interested in personal computers in general, and the Apple II in particular, simply because the machine was the only one on which they could run *VisiCalc* (or, for that matter *any* spreadsheet application).

This led to a significant sales spike for Apple II to serious business users (as opposed to hobbyists, gamers and fledgling programmers, who could be served just as well by the cheaper machines from Commodore, Atari and Radio Shack). By mid-1981, *VisiCalc* had an installed base of more than 100,000. Soon, the release of robust word-processing applications helped goose sales of the Apple II platform ever further within the same market sphere. (Note: While individual hobbyists, gamers, etc. were of course price-sensitive, business purchasers were less so - especially when comparing the price of the Apple II to the cheapest business minis. Thus Apple's higher hardware prices as compared to other small computers, and the relatively expensive cost of software packages such as *VisiCalc*, did not deter expansion within the small business environment.)

Importantly, the Apple II's generous, 8-slot bus architecture allowed for easy expansion of the machine's capabilities. As has been mentioned already, one of the most popular cards offered in 1980 was the SoftCard, from Microsoft, which allowed an Apple II to run CP/M, and thus CP/M compatible software such as the *WordStar* word processor and the *dBase* database management system.

The most popular version of the machine's operating system software was Apple DOS 3.3. In this environment, some commercial Apple II software booted directly from the system and thus did not use standard DOS formats - a sign of other "closed architectures" to come from Apple in the future. This approach discouraged the copying or modifying of software and streamlined the loading process. After Apple DOS came ProDOS, which implemented a hierarchical file-system and thus accommodated larger storage devices. At the height of its evolution, towards the late 1980s, the Apple IIGS would even offer an elementary graphical user interface. And with 16-bit capability at the very end of the Apple II's lifespan (1992's IIe), there would even come a mouse.

*

Apple's strongest competition emerged in August of 1981 with the dawn of the IBM PC. On the heels of IBM's announcement, Apple ran a full-page ad in the *Wall Street Journal* headlined "Welcome IBM. Seriously."

The text continued: "Welcome to the most exciting and important marketplace since the computer revolution began 35 years ago. And congratulations on your first personal computer. Putting real computer power in the hands of the individual is already improving the way people work, think, learn, communicate, and spend their leisure hours. Computer literacy is fast becoming as fundamental a skill as reading or writing. When we invented the first personal computer system, we estimated that over 140,000,000 people worldwide could justify the purchase of one, if only they understood its benefits. Next year alone, we project that well over 1,000,000 will come to that understanding. Over the next decade, the growth of the personal computer will continue in logarithmic leaps. We look forward to responsible competition in the massive effort to distribute this American technology to the world. And we appreciate the magnitude of your commitment. Because what we are doing is increasing social capital by enhancing individual productivity. Welcome to the task. Apple."

At first, the personal computer movement had not threatened - or had not seemed to threaten - IBM's core data processing and office-systems business. But with the rise of machines such as the Apple II, which quickly offered strong word processing, spreadsheet and database management software applications, IBM quite rightly perceived a change in the dynamic. No more did small machines merely represent the sequestered and unprofitable domain of obscure techies, amateur programmers and gamers. The ham radio era of personal computers had ended. The business apps period of these machines was on the rise. In the presence of this looming competition, IBM at last chose to act.

The Intel 8088-based IBM PC (IBM 5150) used 16-bit words to handle data internally, and could handle external communication at 8 bits. The machine included a 62-pin bus, five expansion slots, and used ASCII code. The most stripped down versions of the machine needed no operating system, per se, only BASIC, as it was diskless and featured a cassette port. For those users who wished to incorporate disk storage, they had a choice at first of only the PC-DOS operating system, and later Gary Kildall's more expensive CP/M-86. (The tale of these competing operating systems has, you'll remember, already been told.)

The IBM PC was in many ways better than the Apple II. As Ceruzzi notes: "The monochrome monitor could display a full screen of 25 lines of 80 characters - an improvement over the Apple II and essential for serious office applications. A version with a color monitor was also available. With the PC, IBM also announced the availability of word processing, accounting, games software, and a version of *VisiCalc*. A spreadsheet introduced in October 1982 - *1-2-3* from Mitch Kapor's Lotus Development - took advantage of the PC's architecture and ran much faster than its competitor, *VisiCalc*. The combination of the IBM Personal Computer and Lotus *1-2-3* soon overtook Apple in sales and dispelled whatever doubts remained about these machines as serious rivals to mainframe and minicomputers."

IBM had in fact experimented unsuccessfully with some small computer offerings previous to the PC. Announced in September 1975, the 5100 "Portable Computer" weighted approximately 50 pounds and was targeted to engineers, analysts, and statisticians. IBM made the machine available in 12 different models providing 16K, 32K, 48K or 64K positions of main storage. On the low-end, the 5100 sold for $8,975; on the high end: $19,975. The machine came with either the APL or BASIC programming language, or both. Per IBM's official history: "IBM offered three Problem-Solver Libraries, contained in magnetic tape cartridges, with the IBM 5100 to provide more than 100 interactive routines applicable to mathematical problems, statistical techniques and financial analyses. The cartridge had a 204,000-character capacity on 300 feet of 1/4-inch tape."

Other similar IBM machines rose and fell. Among these was the 5110, launched in 1978 as a fully functional small machine for numerical business use (billing, inventory control, and accounts receivable and sales analysis). Another was the 5520 Administrative System which debuted in late 1979: a dedicated word processor totally focused on the creation, storage, retrieval and editing of documents ranging from single-page memos to multi-page manuals. (Prices for this latter system varied. Per IBM: "For example, a text system with 29 million characters of system/user disk storage capacity, five 5253 display stations and two 5257 printers, cost $64,351 or could be leased for $1,980 a month. A text and document distribution system with 130 million characters of system/user disk storage capacity, fifteen 5253 display stations, six 5257 printers and the necessary features to support communication lines, could be purchased for $175,753 or leased for $5,372 a month.") Additional machines included the IBM DisplayWriter (June 1980).

The groundbreaking aspect of the IBM PC was that it incorporated the functions of all these devices, and more, in a stand-alone platform, and did so at an economical price. At the same time, the machine set much of the standard for personal computing systems going forward throughout its subsequent iterations: the XT and AT models, and the incorporation of hard drives, CD drives and modems. The $1,565 base-price for the original IBM PC bought a system unit, a keyboard and 4-color/graphics capability. Peripheral options included a display, a printer, two floppy diskette drives, extra memory, a communications port, a game adapter and application packages.

For the first time in its history, IBM marketed via such retailers as ComputerLand and Sears as well as IBM sales centers. (Many more retailers signed-on in rapid succession.) To say the least, sales were brisk. By the end of 1982, audited sales actually came in at one system per minute of every business day. Sales at times approached 250,000 units per month. *Newsweek* called the machine a "roaring success." The *New York Times* raved: "The speed and extent to which IBM has been successful has surprised many people, including IBM itself." TIME named the PC "Machine of the Year" for 1983.

But IBM's period of dominance in the sale of PCs was to be short-lived.

IBM Portable Computer, 1975.

Macintosh

> *"The people who are doing the work are the moving force behind the Macintosh. My job is to create a space for them, to clear out the rest of the organization and keep it at bay."*
> - Steve Jobs, co-founder of Apple

Urban legends persist because - despite being untrue - they represent stories that are just too good to let go of. Such is the case with what is widely viewed as a key moment in the history of the development of the Macintosh computer. In a nutshell, the story goes like this: Steve Jobs visited the Xerox Palo Alto Research Center (PARC) in 1979, there saw what Xerox was doing with the development of graphic user interfaces (GUIs), and then lifted the idea (plus several Xerox engineers) for the Mac.

Not true. Jobs did indeed visit Xerox PARC in 1979, but at that time the Macintosh GUI was already very well along and - coincidentally - better than that which was on hand at Xerox. (The Apple paradigm included the "click and drag" method of one-button-mouse-driven function, not a part of the Xerox approach.)

The progenitor of the Macintosh at Apple was Jef [sic] Raskin, a longtime advocate for graphical user interfaces. ("My thesis in *Computer Science*," he recalls, "published in 1967, argued that computers should be all-graphic, that we should eliminate character generators and create characters graphically and in various fonts, that what you see on the screen should be what you get, and that the human interface was more important than mere considerations of algorithmic efficiency and compactness. This was heretical in 1967, half a decade before PARC started.")

During the early 70's Raskin served as professor and computer center director at the University of California, San Diego, and was also Visiting Scholar at the Stanford Artificial Intelligence Laboratory (SAIL). He as well did a stint as visiting academic at Xerox PARC. Raskin had already done much thinking on the design of the user interface for computers, and was delighted to find people at PARC who were on "the same user-interface wavelength." As soon as Raskin joined Apple in 1978, however, he immediately stopped visiting PARC, such visits no longer being appropriate.

Raskin had already known Jobs and Wozniak for two years by the time he was hired as Apple's employee number 31. Raskin, in turn, hired engineer Larry Tesler, one of several PARC veterans to be lured to Apple in the coming months. But far from imitating PARC approaches to GUIs, the new Apple team improved on them dramatically, starting with the invention of the simple one-click mouse as opposed to Xerox's three-click mouse, which often led to confusion and errors on the part of users. Other innovations came rapidly.

"I created this method for moving objects and making selections after finding the Xerox click-move-click method prone to error," writes Raskin. "Bill Atkinson [a former student of Raskin's from the University of California, San Diego who had already developed *QuickDraw* and would go on to create *MacPaint* and *HyperCard* for the Mac] extended the paradigm to pull-down menus. This all happened relatively early in the history of the Mac. The way my insight got extended by Bill was typical of how things developed then. Surprising as it may seem in retrospect, there was some resistance to my new way of using a graphic input device and I had to repeatedly explain how drag worked and why it was often easier to use than the modal click-move-click technique developed first (as far as I know) on the *Sketchpad* system and then used at Xerox PARC. Some of the arguments I used involved looking at the number of user actions and the time they took ... Bill was a strong supporter of my ideas and at one session where I was explaining how drag worked Bill, by way of amplifying how useful it was, said something like, 'And you can use it to open menus, just put the cursor on the top and drag down to the item you want.'"

Raskin's recollection is confirmed by Apple engineer Bruce Horn. "I've been watching the debate for more than a decade now about where the Macintosh User Interface came from," writes Horn. "Most people assume that it was taken directly from Xerox, after Steve Jobs went to visit. This 'fact' is reported over and over, by people who don't know any better (and also by people who should!) This just isn't true - there are some similarities between the Apple interface and the various interfaces on Xerox systems, but the differences are substantial. ... The difference between the Xerox system architectures and the Mac's architecture is huge; much bigger than the difference between the Mac's architecture and Windows. Not surprising, since Microsoft was shown quite a bit of the Macintosh design (API's, sample code, etc.), during the Mac's development from 1981-1984; the intention was to help their programmers write applications for the Mac, but having this also gave their system designers a template from which to start designing Windows. In contrast, the Mac ... designers had to invent their own architectures. Of course, there were some ex-Xerox people ... but the design point for these machines was so different that we didn't leverage off our knowledge of the Xerox systems as much as some people think."

The same went for hardware and packaging. Bruce Horn: "The hardware itself was an amazing step forward ... All-in-one design, 4-voice sound, small footprint, clock, auto-eject floppies, serial ports, and so on. The small, portable, appealing case was a serious departure from the ugly-box-on-an-ugly-box PC world, thanks to Jerry Manock and his crew. Even the packaging showed amazing creativity and passion; do any of you remember unpacking an original 128K Mac? The Mac, the unpacking instructions, the profusely-illustrated and beautifully-written manuals, and the animated practice program with audio cassette were packaged together tastefully in a cardboard box with Picasso-style graphics on the side. Never before had a computer been delivered with so much attention to detail and the customer's needs."

The clear forerunner of the Macintosh was Apple's Lisa - one of the very first GUI-based machines - for which Apple launched development in 1978. According to official Apple history, this name was an acronym for "Local Integrated Software Architecture," though folklore says the machine was named for Steve Jobs' daughter, Lisa, born that year. But per Apple programmer Andy Hertzfeld, the acronym was actually reverse engineered from the name "Lisa" in autumn 1982 by the Apple marketing team. Privately, Hertzfeld and the other developers used "Lisa: Invented Stupid Acronym," which they called a "recursive backronym." Meanwhile, industry pundits went with: "Let's Invent Some Acronym."

When the Lisa issued in 1983 it was pricey at around $10,000 (nevertheless significantly cheaper than its closest competitor, the Xerox Star, released in 1981 with a price of approximately $17,000). Neither machine proved successful. The Lisa sold only an anemic 100,000 units in the course of two years. In addition to its high price as compared to the IBM PC and Apple II, the machine was slow running - this due to an overly large and complex operating system which proved a burden on the 5MHz CPU. Per Ceruzzi: "Raskin's Macintosh would preserve the Lisa's best features but sell at a price that Apple II customers could afford."

Apple introduced the Mac with a still much talked about television commercial directed by Ridley Scott. This

aired in January of 1984 during the Super Bowl. As CNET's
Caroline Murphy recalls: "[The commercial] began, in a
clear nod to George Orwell's novel [*1984*], with tense
strains of music, the image of figures marching through a
tube across a dank industrial complex, and the start of a
bizarre monologue: 'Today we celebrate the first glorious
anniversary of the Information Purification Directives.' ...
Scores of blank-faced people are fixated on a broadcast of a
Big Brother figure on a giant television screen, until a
woman in bright athletic apparel sprints down a center
aisle, wielding a hammer. She hurls it at the screen, which
explodes into a bright white light. The expressions on the
faces in the crowd morph into fascination." Interestingly,
the ad made absolutely no mention of the Mac, and never
showed either the machine or its revolutionary interface.

Priced at $2,495, the first Mac was significantly more
expensive than the IBM PC, but was also obviously a
premium product far above and beyond the PC. As
Ceruzzi writes: "The Mac's elegant system software was its
greatest accomplishment. It displayed a combination of
aesthetic beauty and practical engineering that is
extremely rare." Most importantly, at a time when
computers in general were completely new to most users,
the Macintosh offered an easy, intuitive, non-threatening
interface for deploying and maximizing powerful business
applications.

Although the hardware was expensive as compared to
the PC, employers could count on considerably fewer
man-hours being spent by novice "virgin" users getting up

to speed on the desktop. It is important to remember that this was a time well before the advent of Microsoft Windows, when much of the power a PC offered was delivered via an arcane DOS C:/ prompt which demanded the absolute correct keying of commands, directory and file locations in order to open applications and file locations, or the use of DOS shells which were themselves not much more friendly.

The same went for powerful and popular PC applications such as Lotus *1-2-3*, *WordStar* (published by MicroPro International), Corel's *WordPerfect*, and a host of DBMS (database management system) software packages. Employing obtuse commands and procedures, and coming with only the briefest documentation, these early PC applications proved to be uniquely user-*unfriendly*. In fact, they fostered a very lucrative side-business of book publishers providing user-manuals and reference works. Small start-ups such as Que Publishing grew quickly into multimillion dollar enterprises. Others included an imprint started by Adam Osborne (this eventually sold to McGraw-Hill), as well as Sybex, Ventana Press, Peachpit Press, MIS Press, and others. Macintosh apps from Microsoft and other providers were, however, customized to maximize the machine's easy, intuitive interface, and were in many ways "self-documenting."

Macs were also a good way to avoid a score of inefficiencies, deficiencies and errors of omission apparent in the PC's operating system, now called MS-DOS. These shortcomings had, in 1982, led to the release of what became known as the *Norton Utilities*, designed by programmer Peter Norton. Priced at $80, the Utilities included an *UnErase* feature which allowed files to be undeleted, as well as 13 more vital (and, one would think, obvious) tools not available within DOS proper, including *FileFix* for repairing damaged files and *DiskLook* for easily surveying the contents and maps of floppies. (After many, many releases and revisions, the Norton Utilities remain a very popular set of tools. Peter Norton sold his company to the software firm Symantec in 1990.)

The PC would - especially after the advent of cheaper and better clones (see next chapter), and the advent of the intuitive Windows user interface - remain dominant with those business users most concerned with spreadsheeting, word processing and database management. However, the Macintosh would remain always a very strong second in the business landscape, especially with regards to graphically-intensive packages such as desktop page design applications, drawing applications, multimedia development and such.

Steve Jobs won a dubious reward for his triumph with the Macintosh. After losing a power struggle with the board of directors in 1984, he resigned from Apple and founded NeXT, a computer platform development company meant to specialize in products for the higher education and business markets, especially the former. NeXT proved only marginal successful. Eventually, in 1996, Apple bought NeXT, thus bringing Jobs back to the company he co-

founded, and to his one true calling. He served as CEO near
his death in October of 2011.

Bring on the Clones

*"A computer lets you make more mistakes faster than any
invention in human history - with the possible exceptions of
handguns and tequila."*
- Mitch Ratcliffe, programmer

From the start, the Macintosh was a "closed"
architecture. Unlike the PC or the Apple II, there were no
slots for users to add boards or otherwise customize the
hardware. There were also to be no clones of this or any
other Apple machine, because Apple controlled all rights
to its operating system and held patents on the vast
majority of Macintosh parts. Going forward, Apple was
always to remain the sole purveyor of any of its hardware
products, as well as its operating systems, thus dictating
prices for the market.

Not so with regard to the IBM PC, for which IBM
owned only the rudimentary BIOS input/output code. IBM
had no exclusivity in its license for MS-DOS. As well, the
PC was made up of parts from other manufacturers for
which IBM held no exclusive rights. Thus competitors
were free to reverse engineer their own versions of the PC
to run MS-DOS so long as they devised their own BIOS
code, which was not hard to do.

The first out of the gate was a machine from a new
firm called Compaq (acronym for *Compatibility and*

Quality), formed in 1982 by three former Texas Instruments engineers: Rod Canion, Jim Harris and Bill Murto. The "Compaq Portable" emerged in 1983 - a machine capable of doing everything the PC could, running precisely the same software, but considerably smaller - so much so that it gained the slang name "suitcase computer." This was rapidly followed by Compaq's aggressively priced "DeskPro" line of desktop computers. Per Ceruzzi: "What made it a success was its complete compatibility with the IBM PC at a competitive price. Compaq's sales propelled the company into the top 100 rankings of computer companies by 1985, one of the fastest trajectories of any start-up." Compaq would go on to be acquired by another clone-maker, Hewlett-Packard, in 2002 - at a price of $25 billion.

At first, few clones other than Compaq's offered full compatibility. The ability to run Lotus *1-2-3* or *Microsoft Flight Simulator* became a standard stress test employed by reviewers and users. Soon, Phoenix Technologies developed an IBM-compatible BIOS available for license - enabling virtually anyone to build a 100% compatible clone without any R&D whatsoever. Thus other clones soon followed from such new firms as Michael Dell's PCs Limited - firms which were to log far more unit-sales than would IBM through the years.

After Compaq, Dell's firm turned into the most significant of all clone makers. As a student at the University of Texas, Austin, Michael Dell launched PCs Limited out of his dorm room in 1984. Later, after borrowing about $300,000 in start-up capital from his family, Dell dropped out of school in order to pursue his business full-time.

The company produced its first computer - the "Turbo PC", selling for $795 - in 1985. All of PCs Limited's sales were direct to consumers, the machines being marketed through ads in computer magazines. Each unit shipped custom built according to a given purchaser's selection of menu items (a unique service exclusive to PCs Limited, one made possible by their shunning of retail distribution). Direct selling also enabled the firm to price their PCs at a sharp discount to the prices available through retailers for clones from other manufacturers while at the same time assuring themselves a greater per-unit margin than what their competitors enjoyed.

The company grossed more than $73 million in 1986, changed its name to Dell Computer Corporation in 1988, then began expanding overseas. In the course of one week in June of 1988, Dell's market capitalization grew by $30 million to $80 million from its June 22 initial public offering of 3.5 million shares at $8.50 a share. Four years later, *Fortune* added Dell to its list of the world's 500 largest companies. This made Michael Dell the all-time youngest CEO of a *Fortune 500* firm.

Adding to the demise of IBM's own PC sales (vs. clones) was the fact that IBM itself failed to understand the importance of "IBM compatibility." Such products as the IBM Portable (outperformed, out-priced and outsold by the earlier Compaq Portable) and the PCjr (flawed by significant incompatibilities with the original PC) alienated many users, and further encouraged the turn toward clone-makers. Through the years, releases of PC hardware by clone manufacturers were always to directly mirror new releases and enhancements of the original PC from IBM - including the XT of 1983, and the second-generation AT ("Advanced Technology") designed around the 80286 chip, released 1984.

"Of course, IBM no longer makes PCs," comments *PC World* contributing editor Lincoln Spector. "In the mid-1980s the company attempted to take back control of the standard with a significant upgrade - the Micro Channel Architecture PS/2, which was software-compatible, but not hardware-compatible, with the PC. However, it was Compaq, the first and largest of the clone manufacturers, that offered the upgrade everyone really wanted: a PC based on Intel's 32-bit 80386 processor. Big Blue remained a major player in the PC market throughout the 1990s, but it was no longer the biggest player. During that time it concentrated on its ThinkPad notebooks rather than desktop PCs. In 2005 IBM sold its PC division, including the ThinkPad, to the Lenovo Group."

Elsewhere he writes: "With their beautiful graphics, multitasking applications, and networking talents, today's gigahertz-plus systems seem a far cry from the PCs of two decades ago. Still, at the heart of every 21st century Windows-based computer lies an IBM PC." The bootstrapping of evolution requires antecedents, all of whom leave their indelible mark. As Mitch Kapor has recently noted: at least 98% of the DNA for today's PCs comes from that original and now seemingly-ancient machine first released in 1981.

Proliferation of clone-makers of course fueled aggressive price-competition, which in turn helped build a staggeringly high installed-base of PC-compatible machines throughout industry in a relatively short period of time. By 1987, the installed base of PC-compatible machines was over 9 million - this for a platform that had only been first launched six years earlier. The lion's share of these were clones.

The big winner, of course, was Microsoft, which supplied the operating system for each and every machine in that massive and rapidly growing installed base. Firms like Dell and Compaq each held significant pieces of the hardware action in the PC-compatible marketplace. But Microsoft held ALL the action as regards the operating system and - as we shall see - much of the most relevant software as well.

On November 20, 1984, while in the midst of working jointly with IBM on the creation of OS/2 (tied to IBM's doomed next generation PC called PS/2), Microsoft released Microsoft Windows, the firm's graphical extension for MS-DOS. Ala the Macintosh, the Windows operating system incorporated drop-down menus, scroll bars, icons, and dialog boxes that made programs easier to learn and use. Importantly, Windows made it possible to switch among several programs without having to quit and restart each one. Version 1.0 shipped with several

programs, including MS-DOS file management, *Paint,*
Windows Writer, Notepad, Calculator, and a calendar, card
file, and clock to help users manage day-to-day activities.
The operating system would be constantly revised and
enhanced by Microsoft through the years, and of course
still remains dominant on the PC platform to this very day.

Fifteen months after the release of Windows 1.0,
Microsoft went public. The ensuing rise in the stock
created four billionaires and approx. 12,000 Microsoft
employee millionaires.

Intrigued by Microsoft's close relationship with IBM,
in 1990 the Federal Trade Commission began investigating
Microsoft for possible collusion in the PC marketplace.
Had the regulators understood anything about PC
operating systems, they might not have bothered. At the
same time that the investigation was launched, Microsoft
engineers were at work on a 32-bit OS, Microsoft Windows
NT, which used ideas from OS/2 but improved on them
and was meant to help short-circuit IBM's ambitions for
both OS/2 and the PS/2. Windows NT shipped on July 21,
1993. Incorporating a new modular kernel and the elegant
Win32 application programming interface (API), the
operating system greatly simplified porting from 16-bit
(MS-DOS-based) Windows to more powerful machines. In
the midst of this, IBM's ambitions for both OS/2 and the
PS/2 computer quickly collapsed, and Microsoft became
ever more dominant in the operating system space.

At the same time, key Microsoft applications products
- most notably *Microsoft Word* and *Microsoft Excel* (the latter

for spreadsheeting) - remained market-leaders on both the PC and Macintosh platforms, circumventing apps such as *WordStar, WordPerfect* and Lotus *1-2-3*. (In 1990 Microsoft launched *Microsoft Office*, a bundle of their most popular productivity applications, including *Word* and *Excel*.)

Not finding collusion with IBM, the U.S. Department of Justice sought out other Microsoft violations of fair trade, either real or imagined. Microsoft and the Justice Department were to spar more than once.

Networks

"There are only two industries that refer to their customers as 'users'."
- Edward Tufte, statistician, discussing both the computer business and the illicit drug trade

At first, the entire emphasis of personal computing had of course been on the "personal" aspect of the technology - to each his own independent machine: utter and complete independence and freedom. This had been the philosophy which arose out of the hobbyist clubs where the small machines first spread their roots. But business users had other needs, wants and desires, not the least of which were the economies to be achieved with shared use of key computer resources and communication between machines. Thus the rise of Local Area Networks (LANS) which, in contrast to Wide Area Networks (WANs), offer higher data-transfer rates, are usually confined to one office or set of offices, and do not require leased telecommunication lines.

The world's first commercially available LAN was installed in September 1977 at the New York offices of Chase Manhattan Bank. ARCnet (Attached Resource Computer Network) was developed by Datapoint Corporation in San Antonio, Texas. Designed by a team led by John Murphy, with operating system code written by Gordon Peterson, ARCnet was defined as a group of nodes that communicate over a geographically-limited area usually within one building or, at most, a campus of buildings. To this day, ARCnet represents the simplest, most economical type of LAN. It uses what is called a token-ring architecture, supports data rates of 2.5 Mbps, and connects up to 255 computers. At the time, ARCnet's most radical innovation was that it allowed various types of transmission media to be mixed on the same network: twisted-pair wire (maximum extension 150 meters), coaxial cable (650 m.) and fiber optic cable (2.000 m.).

"I worked for Chase Manhattan Bank from 1976 until 1986," comments veteran computer engineer Chris Piggot, "and was one of the first to use the ARC in a live commercial environment. I remember Gordon Peterson, Jonathan Schmidt and others at Datapoint well. ARC allowed Datapoint to 'punch far above its weight' when compared to the IBM, DEC and Wang alternatives at the time. Not bad considering its eight bit architecture. The first system we developed using ARC was a funds transfer system connected to the New York Clearing House, processing thousands of transactions per day, worth tens of billions dollars. At its peak, Chase had scores of individual networks installed, some with 20 or more linked processors."

Previously there had been several successful non-commercial LANs set up in various educational institutions and research labs. By 1970 the Lawrence Radiation Laboratory had an in-house "Octopus" network up and running. Shortly thereafter, in 1974, Cambridge Ring was developed at Cambridge University. However, neither of these implementations ever morphed into a commercial product.

As has been so often the case in the development of all aspects of commercial computing, ARCnet was in many ways out of date from a R&D point view well before its installation at Chase. During the years 1973 - 1975, engineers at Xerox PARC designed what they called the "Ethernet," a "packet switch" network which they installed for use at the PARC in 1976. Ethernet offered the appeal of being device- and operating system-neutral, allowing any number of different platforms - such as PC-compatibles and Macs - to share network resources.

In the small computer marketplace of business users, integration of multiple differing platforms was at first inhibited by the distribution of "closed" machine- and operating system-specific networking products such as AppleTalk, which shipped with the first generation of Macintosh machines.

The first commercial Ethernet solution to this problem came in the form of Novell NetWare. Initially released in 1983, this networking product was to remain dominant well into the 1990s, at which point its prominence would end in the face of Microsoft's Windows NT Advanced Server and Windows for Workgroups.

Founded in 1979 by veterans of Provo, Utah's Eyring Research Institute (ERI), Novell is today a subsidiary of

The Attachmate Group. Throughout its life, the firm has focused on enterprise operating systems such as NetWare, upon which its initial fortunes were based. Per Novell's own corporate literature: "Novell helped invent the corporate network in the early 1980s and continues to drive technology for business today. Network software began with the sharing of files and printers within local area networks (LANs) and evolved into the management of wide area networks that enabled enterprise-class computing and, ultimately, the Internet."

The NetWare network operating system enabled cooperative multitasking using network protocols based on the Xerox Network Systems stack. NetWare evolved from a very simple concept: file sharing instead of disk sharing. LAN products had, up until the release of NetWare, been based on the concept of providing shared direct disk access: disk sharing. As of 1984, when IBM endorsed Novell's alternative approach of file sharing as opposed to disk sharing, NetWare came for a time to own the small computer networking marketplace, being the preferred network operating system for the sharing of files and peripherals and the linking of machines for that new, radical inter-office tool called "e-mail."

In 1988, *InfoWorld* pointed out that shipments of token-ring networks (such as ARCnet) were in "sharp ascent" while Ethernets represented some 78% of the total network operating systems installed base, with NetWare Ethernets at almost 70%. Per an official Novell statement on its history: "Novell developed a PC networking system that designated one machine to manage the network and control access to shared devices, such as disk drives and printers. Through the 1980s, corporate requirements for networks grew significantly, with LANs being increasingly replaced by wide area networks, which unified large corporate environments. By the early 1990s, Novell's NetWare operating system, updated to add key features for distributed enterprises, led this market with a nearly 70 % share. In 1996, recognizing that the Internet was beginning to revolutionize the traditional network market, interim CEO John Young initiated a program to make the company's products Internet ready." (In fact, NetWare provided limited support for TCP/IP, the backbone of the Internet, as early as 1992, although it would not incorporate native TCP/IP support for client and print services until NetWare 5.0, released 1998.)

Other firms were also preparing for the Internet. On May 26, 1995, Bill Gates issued a now-famous memo to all Microsoft executive staff members entitled "The Internet Tidal Wave." In this document, Gates laid out what he saw on the horizon, and his thinking on how Microsoft should prepare for the next great revolution in the digital realm.

"Our vision for the last 20 years can be summarized in a succinct way," Gates wrote. "We saw that exponential improvements in computer capabilities would make great software quite valuable. Our response was to build an organization to deliver the best software products. In the next 20 years the improvement in computer power will be outpaced by the exponential improvements in communications networks. The combination of these elements will have a fundamental impact on work, learning and play. Great software products will be crucial to delivering the benefits of these advances. Both the variety and volume of the software will increase."

Gates continued: "Most users of communications have not yet seen the price of communications come down significantly. Cable and phone networks are still depreciating networks built with old technology. Universal service monopolies and other government involvement around the world have kept communications costs high. Private networks and the Internet which are built using state of the art equipment have been the primary beneficiaries of the improved communications technology. The PC is just now starting to create additional demand that will drive a new wave of investment. A combination of expanded access to the Internet, ISDN, new broadband networks justified by video based applications and interconnections between each of these will bring low cost communication to most businesses and homes within the next decade. The Internet is at the forefront of all of this and developments on the Internet over the next several years will set the course of our industry for a long time to come. Perhaps you have already seen memos from me or others here about the importance of the Internet. I have gone through several stages of increasing my views of its importance. Now I assign the Internet the highest level of importance. In this memo I want to make clear that our focus on the Internet is crucial to every part of our business. The Internet is the most important single

development to come along since the IBM PC was
introduced in 1981. It is even more important than the
arrival of the graphical user interface (GUI). The PC
analogy is apt for many reasons. The PC wasn't perfect.
Aspects of the PC were arbitrary or even poor. However a
phenomena grew up around the IBM PC that made it a
key element of everything that would happen for the next
15 years. Companies that tried to fight the PC standard
often had good reasons for doing so but they failed
because the phenomena overcame any weaknesses that
resisters identified."

*

The online world of PC users had up to now been
restricted to a few proprietary subscription digital
environments such as CompuServe and Prodigy.

Compu-Serv Network, Inc. was launched in 1969; and
its inspiration was serendipitous. An Ohio-based
insurance company (Golden United Life Insurance) found
itself in a position where, in order to completely serve its
computing needs, it had to buy a DEC machine of
oversized capacity. Executives, in turn, decided to lease
out the machine's excess.

For nine years - in a model resembling today's cloud
computing paradigm - customers were strictly corporate.
But as of 1978 the firm began to market to the small but

growing population of small computer owners. 3,600 users had enrolled in the service by 1980.

That same year, the firm - now "CompuServe" - began making newspaper content available online. AP President and General Manager Keith Fuller is quoted as saying: "Since the newspapers began providing their electronic editions to CompuServe, CompuServe has grown from 3,600 subscribers in mid-1980 to more than 10,000 in the first quarter of 1981." But in fact newspaper readers accounted for only 5% of CompuServe's usage.

Growth became exponential. By early 1984, CompuServe boasted more than 60,000 subscribers. These subscribers paid an access fee of 13 cents per minute during the day and 10 cents a minute at night. They spent their time in topic-specific chat rooms, exchanged e-mail, read online content, and eventually shopped in the stores of a "CompuServe Mall." Most of the service's users were computer nerds, and most of the service's topic forums were technical in nature.

The fastest modems? 300 bps. At least at first. The interface? Entirely text and menu driven. At least at first.

During 1986, the tax return preparation firm H&R Block purchased CompuServe for $23 million: a very wise investment. CompuServe grew faster than any other Block division. By the end of the fiscal year which closed at the end of April 1989, CompuServe was contributing $68 million to Block's sales (approx. 15% of total revenues) and almost $8 million in operating profits.

In that same year, CompuServe's only relevant competitor was The Source, a consumer online service based in McLean, Virginia. Block bought The Source in June of 1989, ported its 53,000 subscribers to CompuServe, and shut down the Source service on August 1. Eventually, CompuServe was expanded into Europe and beyond. By 1993, 90,000 of its more than 1.5 million subscribers were in Europe. But the market was quickly growing beyond programmers and hardware buffs, and competition rose up.

In 1997, H&R Block announced its intention to sell off CompuServe. The up-and coming America Online, the most logical buyer, made several offers to purchase CompuServe using AOL stock, but Block management sought cash. Early in 1998, John W. Sidgmore, vice-chairman of WorldCom and former CEO of UUNET, contrived a complicated, elegant transaction which met the needs and capabilities of all parties, while also playing out to WorldCom's advantage. WorldCom acquired all the shares of CompuServe using $1.2 billion of WorldCom stock. As previously arranged, Block nearly immediately sold the WorldCom stock to other investors for $1.2 billion in cash. Also as previously arranged, within one day of this deal, WorldCom sold the Information Service portion of CompuServe to AOL, retaining for itself the CompuServe Network Services portion. At the same time, AOL sold its networking division, Advanced Network Services (ANS), to WorldCom. Business analysts praised the deal as a beautiful construct: AOL was doing information services; WorldCom was doing networks;

Block had been properly recompensed; and all felt as if they'd driven a profitable bargain.

Now CompuServe Network Services was combined with ANS and an existing WorldCom networking enterprise called Gridnet to form WorldCom Advanced Networks. (Meanwhile CompuServe remained a discrete brand under the AOL umbrella.) One year after the CompuServe deal, WorldCom acquired MCI and became MCI WorldCom; WorldCom Advanced Networks in turn became MCI WorldCom Advanced Networks and - after a failed bid by WorldCom to acquire Sprint - was rolled into UUNET. After a much-publicized bankruptcy, WorldCom emerged as MCI which, in 2006, was sold to Verizon.

The buyer of CompuServe Information Services, AOL, had been founded by Steve Case and Jim Kimsey as Quantum Computer Services in 1985. The concept behind Quantum was to provide online services (QuantumLink, or Q-Link for short) for users of the then-popular and highly-economical Commodore computers. "The idea was that someday people would want to be able to interact and get stock quotes and talk with other people or all these different things," Case has recalled. "I just believed that was going to happen." Elsewhere he has said: "If you're doing something new you've got to have a vision. You've got to have a perspective. You've got to have some north star you're aiming for, and you just believe somehow you'll get there, which kind of gets to the passion point."

In 1987, with the Commodore installed base declining in comparison to the growth of the Apple II and Macintosh machines, Case and Kimsey opened up their service to be compatible with Apple operating systems. Following this innovation, Quantum grew quickly and was soon providing online services and related software for other companies, including Tandy Corporation and IBM.

Quantum's costs were high, and it quickly ran through its capital. The proprietors rebranded Quantum as *America Online* (AOL) in 1989, and reorganized with Case taking Kimsey's place as CEO and Kimsey becoming chairman. AOL held its initial public offering in March 1992 and raised $66 million, shares initially selling for $1.64.

At that time, the two leaders in providing online services were Prodigy (to be discussed shortly) and, as previously noted, CompuServe. Post-IPO, Case invested aggressively in the expansion of AOL. He developed a beautiful user interface, set subscription prices well below those of his competition, and filled the mailboxes of subscribers to consumer-based computer-related publications with diskettes providing AOL connection software. The software came with a free trial offer. This smart marketing resulted in rapid growth. By the end of 1993 the company had more than 600,000 subscribers.

AOL found itself the subject of two unfriendly takeover attempts in 1993. The first came from Microsoft cofounder Paul Allen (now departed from that firm), the other from Microsoft. Allen eventually acquired a 24.9 percent interest in AOL but was denied a seat on the board. Case successfully fought off both attempts, leaving

Allen to pursue other ventures and Microsoft to eventually create its own online service, the Microsoft Network.

At the time of its 2001 merger with Time Warner, AOL's capitalization sat at a $240 billion high. But it was all downhill from there, largely - of course - due to the rise of the open Internet and Web as a borderless online universe. AOL's subscriber base saw no quarterly growth from 2002 onward.

As of 2011, things seem even bleaker. "In the two years since he took over [AOL Chairman Tim] Armstrong has succeeded in spinning off AOL from its former parent, Time Warner, ending a ten-year union that's widely viewed as one of the most disastrous in corporate history," wrote journalist Tim Bercovici in a spring 2011 edition of *Forbes*. "But that doesn't mean it has left the past behind. The company is still reliant on its rapidly declining Internet-access business, which charges 3.6 million subscribers (down from 4.1 million last September) an average $18 a month and was responsible, directly or indirectly, for more than 40% of the company's $551 million first-quarter revenues. An aggressive plan to rebrand AOL as a provider of original content has yet to pay off in meaningful traffic or advertising growth. Patch, a network of 800-plus local news websites that Armstrong helped to found and then had AOL acquire in 2009, is blowing through $40 million a quarter without generating meaningful revenue. Armstrong promises AOL's display-advertising business, the focus of his strategy, will soon be growing at industry-average rates of around 20% per year, but so far the best he's clocked is a meager 4%." At the same time, few analysts see AOL's recent $315 million acquisition of the *Huffington Post* as a game-changer.

Another player in the subscription online service market was Prodigy, founded in 1984 by Trintex, a joint venture between CBS, IBM and Sears. CBS left the partnership in 1986. Formally launched in 1988 after four years of R&D, by 1990 the Prodigy service hosted 465,000 users, second only to CompuServe (600,000).

The service provided real-time news, games, and e-mail, but was slow to offer the type of perks that quickly helped AOL supersede all other players, such as anonymous handles, real-time chat, and unmoderated discussion-boards. In the early 1990s, strapped for cash-flow, Prodigy limited monthly e-mail messages to thirty, after which a surcharge applied; then in the summer of 1993 Prodigy began charging hourly rates for its most popular features, including message boards. Although later rescinded, these policies caused thousands of subscribers to leave the service, most of these heading for AOL, which offered a sexier interface and reliable service while at the same providing better processing and more attractive pricing.

By the early 1990s, all the dial-ups were offering such services as online banking, online stock trading, and various shopping options. Notably, however, in 1994 Prodigy became the first of the early-generation dialup services to offer full access to the World Wide Web, as well as Web page hosting, to its members, along with access to

USENET newsgroups. CompuServe and AOL soon
followed with similar approaches. Ultimately, however,
the Internet was to quickly gain on Prodigy just as it
would all of the old dial-up players.

In 1996, IBM and Sears sold their interests in Prodigy
to the newly founded International Wireless, with Mexican
businessman Carlos Slim Helu (a principal owner of
Telmex) as minority investor. IBM and Sears took a bath
on the transaction. The sales price was $200 million.
Between them, the sellers had invested more than $1
billion in the service since 1984. In due course, Prodigy
developed high-speed Internet capability, and in 2000 SBC
(Southwestern Bell Company, as of 2006 AT&T) bought a
43% interest. The firm - now with a division called Prodigy
Broadband - took on the task of servicing SBC's 77 million
high-speed Internet customers. Eventually SBC bought
controlling interest for $465 million. At the time, Prodigy
ranked as the fourth-largest Internet service provider
behind AOL, Microsoft's MSN, and EarthLink. In the year
2000, Prodigy logged 3.1 million subscribers, of which 1.3
million were DSL users. Nevertheless, the Prodigy brand
was eventually put into defacto retirement. Users who
sought Prodigy on the Internet found themselves
redirected to att.net.

By far the coolest online community, however, was the
WELL (Whole Earth 'Lectronic Link), launched in 1985
by *Whole Earth Catalog* founder Stewart Brand along with
partner Larry Brilliant. The WELL started life as a simple
dial-up bulletin board system (BBS), but in the early 1990s

became one of the original dial-up ISPs. Today it remains a popular community destination on the Internet.

The WELL's early management team - Matthew McClure, Cliff Figallo and John Coate - collaborated closely with users to foster a sense of virtual community. In 1994, the founders sold the WELL to Bruce Katz (the entrepreneur behind Rockport, maker of walking shoes), who owned the enterprise till 1999. Since the spring of that year, the WELL has been owned by Salon.com. For many years, the WELL was a central digital gathering place for Deadheads, and always maintained a counter-culture feel. Importantly, many major thinkers and technologists concerned with the present and future of online communications found a home for their early discussions on the WELL. For example, technologist Harold Rheingold took inspiration from the WELL to create his now classic book *The Virtual Community*.

"The virtual village of a few hundred people I stumbled upon in 1985 grew to eight thousand by 1993," Rheingold recalled. "It became clear to me during the first months of that history that I was participating in the self-design of a new kind of culture. I watched the community's social contracts stretch and change as the people who discovered and started building the WELL in its first year or two were joined by so many others. Norms were established, challenged, changed, reestablished, rechallenged, in a kind of speeded-up social evolution." Speeded-up indeed.

AutoDesk, Adobe Systems and Other Success Stories

"Software is a great combination between artistry and engineering. When you finally get done and get to appreciate what you have done it is like a part of yourself that you've put together. I think a lot of the people here feel that way."
- Bill Gates, co-founder of Microsoft

The rise of the dominant word processing, spreadsheeting and database applications have already been discussed in this narrative. A number of other software categories, and software developers, need to be acknowledged. First among these is AutoDesk.

Founded in 1982 by John Walker and fourteen other engineers, AutoDesk first found success with *AutoCad* - the firm's flagship product - released 1982. This computer-aided-design (CAD) application was to become wildly popular among architects and engineers. The app was configured to run on microcomputers running the 8-bit CP/M operating system, as well as two 16-bit systems: the short-lived Victor 9000 and the IBM PC. *AutoCAD* enabled the easy creation of detailed technical drawings, and was priced so as to be attractive to smaller design, engineering, and architecture firms. The real focus from the start, however, was on the IBM PC.

"We arrived just at the time that the IBM PC had turned the whole PC business upside down," recalls Walker. "Suddenly you had this completely new machine, which could not run any of the existing software written for the Z-80 and CP/M, you had 15-20 manufacturers jumping in the market with both feet ... boatloads of these PCs with absolutely no software to run on it, other than CP/M or MS-DOS. And quickly-ported and ghastly versions of *WordStar* and so forth, which were mostly hack-ported from CP/M and kinda worked, maybe. And there was this huge vacuum awaiting software ... that was the whole concept of the company: we are at a juncture here. There are millions of these machines coming in that need software. They are not going to sell unless they have software on them. And we - fifteen mainframe programmers - know how to build big software packages. And further, we're familiar with the applications that run on mainframes, and these machines in a couple of years are going to have the power of mainframes and will need mainframe-style software."

Walker continues: "Back then, at the point we launched *AutoCAD* at COMDEX, that was the work of three people over about six or seven months. The manual was written by one guy - the original manual, which I don't have - didn't have any illustrations in it. It's the manual of a CAD program, and it didn't have any pictures in it, because we didn't have any way to make them then. *AutoCAD* didn't work well enough, hardly, to get the pictures in the manual! It was printed out on a daisywheel printer; that's how the master was made. And so you didn't need venture capital when you had people - who, at that point, were pretty senior people in their regular jobs - moonlighting and able to throw something like that together."

Release 2.1 of *AutoCAD* (1986) incorporated a powerful built-in Lisp interpreter, *AutoLISP*, designed to empower third party developers to extend AutoCAD's functionality, thus helping AutoDesk make its product especially appealing to a wide range of vertical markets ranging from landscape designers to ship builders. Effective with Release 14 (1997), AutoDesk configured the product exclusively for Microsoft Windows (abandoning the SUN UNIX workstation, Macintosh and other platforms).

Walker: "It was only after Carol Bartz [who became CEO of AutoDesk in 1992] arrived that the winnowing of platforms started. I think we may even still have had the Macintosh version then. Maybe, maybe not. But we definitely had Sun, HP Apollo, and SGI, still. MicroVAX had basically petered out, as DEC had abandoned the MicroVAX. Somebody was working on a NeXT - I don't think that ever got done. But the radical focusing on Windows and Windows NT was really something of the Bartz era. And let me say - that was something I was 100% vehemently for ... I was onboard with that."

To this day, *AutoCAD* remains the most widely accepted and used program for 2D and 3D modeling. At the same time, several of AutoDesk's native file formats are the most widely used for CAD data interoperability.

After its purchase of Softdesk in 1997, AutoDesk started to develop specialty versions of *AutoCAD* customized for architects, civil engineers, etc. Concurrently, the company began to develop and offer a number of powerful non-*AutoCAD*-based products, including *Revit*, a parametric building modeling application (acquired in 2002, from Massachusetts-based Revit Technologies for $133 million), and *Inventor*, an internally developed parametric mechanical design CAD application.

AutoDesk went public in 1985 with a 1.6 million share IPO priced at $11.00 per share. In March 2008 AutoDesk was named number 25 on *Fast Company's* list of "The World's 50 Most Innovative Companies." In October 2010, AutoDesk returned to the Apple market with *AutoCAD for Mac*. As of this writing, the firm has annual revenue of $1.952 billion and 6,800 employees.

Adobe Systems represented another major software success story.

Founded in Silicon Valley by Xerox PARC vets John Warnock and Charles Geschke in 1982, Adobe took its name from Adobe Creek in Los Altos, California, which ran behind the house of one of the founders.

Adobe's first order of business was to develop and market the *PostScript* page description language, subsequently licensed to Apple in 1985 for use in that firm's LaserWriter printers. In turn, as the Mac and LaserWriter became integral to the art and practice of desktop publishing (DTP), so too did *PostScript*. Licensing royalties poured in, funding vital R&D on which Adobe's future fortunes would be based.

Adobe's next foray was into digital fonts, which the firm released in a proprietary format called *Type 1*. Shortly, after Apple developed (and licensed to Microsoft) the rival standard *TrueType* (powering full scalability and precise control of the pixel pattern created by font outlines) Adobe returned fire by publishing the *Type 1* specification, thus allowing third-party developers to enter the game. At the same time, Adobe released *Adobe Type Manager*. Though it lacked pixel-level control, this latter software nevertheless allowed WYSIWYG (What You See Is What You Get) scaling of fonts on screen just like *TrueType*.

In the end, *TrueType* endured to dominate the general software market, becoming a core element of Windows. *Type 1*, however, came to own the small, but still lucrative, graphics/publishing market. Eventually, Microsoft and Adobe hammered out a truce and in 1996 announced the *OpenType* font format (fully implemented by 2003).

During the mid-1980s, Adobe entered the DTP software market with *Adobe Illustrator for the Macintosh*, a vector-based drawing application. Far more elegant than Apple's own *MacDraw*, *Illustrator* provided nearly perfect WYSIWYG accuracy. Following this, in 1989, Adobe released what was to become its flagship product: the *Photoshop* graphics editing package. Four years later, Adobe introduced the Portable Document Format (PDF) -

still today the worldwide standard for electronic documents and the revolutionary Adobe Acrobat Reader.

Adobe was slow to address the emerging Windows DTP market, although it eventually had a measure of success in this space with *InDesign* and the bundled *Creative Suite*. One other misstep was Adobe's costly development and release of a version of *Illustrator* for Steve Jobs' ill-fated NeXT system, along with a poorly-implemented version for Windows.

Adobe released *Adobe Premiere* in December of 1989, this to be rebranded as *Adobe Premiere Pro* in 2003. During 1984, Adobe acquired Aldus, thus adding *PageMaker* and *After Effects* to its portfolio; Adobe as well controls the vital TIFF file format. In 1995, Adobe added *FrameMaker*, a robust long-document DTP application, to its portfolio after acquiring Frame Technology Corp. During 1999, Adobe introduced Adobe *InCopy* as a direct competitor to *QuarkCopyDesk*. Many more acquisitions and software releases were to follow.

Adobe Systems went public, entering the NASDAQ, in 1986. Adobe's 2006 revenues were reported as $2.575 billion. As of this writing (spring 2011), Adobe's market capitalization stands at approximately $17 billion.

Other success stories include systems-security provider Symantec, founded in 1984 with a National Science Foundation grant and now a *Fortune 500* company and a member of the S&P 500 stock market index. Approximately two-thirds of the company's revenue comes from the design and distribution of enterprise software, with the balance being security and optimization apps and utilities for PCs and Apple products.

One must also mention Oracle Corporation, founded in 1977 by Larry Ellison, Bob Miner and Ed Oates. The firm has long specialized in creating and distributing enterprise software, especially database management systems, and recently moved into hardware. Oracle went public in 1986 with revenues of $55 million. At the end of 2006, Oracle boasted the world's third-largest software revenue, trailing only Microsoft and IBM. Best known for its *Oracle Database*, the firm also concentrates on middle-tier software, enterprise resource planning (ERP), and CRM and SCM software. Larry Ellison has remained at the firm's helm all these years, serving as CEO up to the present writing and, until 2006, as Chairman of the Board.

"I've run engineering since day one at Oracle, and I still run engineering," Ellison told an interviewer in 2006. "I hold meetings every week with the database team, the middleware team, the applications team. I run engineering, and I will do that until the board throws me out of there. I'm also involved with all of the acquisitions and overall strategy. Now it's true, I don't run operations. But I've never really run operations. I've never had the endurance to run sales. The whole idea of selling to the customer just isn't my personality. I'm an engineer - tell me why something isn't working or is, and I'm curious."

In the first decade of this century, Ellison launched a strenuous program of strategic acquisitions. "The company

is already dominating the market in database software,"
commented a journalist in 2006, "and Ellison is determined
to beat his rivals in applications and middleware: the
software that sits between a computer's operating system
(such as Windows) and its applications (such as *Word*). To
do this he has embarked upon an extraordinarily
ambitious shopping spree, spending close to $20 billion
dollars on 21 companies over the past 18 months. Some
acquisitions have been land grabs, such as the hostile
takeover of PeopleSoft or the friendlier purchase of Siebel.
Others were for particular technologies and engineers.
And Ellison's voracious appetite continues unabated. At
the moment he is looking to buy industry specific software
to overtake Oracle's greatest rival, Germany's SAP, in
applications. Speculation is rife as to his next target."

Eventually, in 2009, Ellison would surprise virtually
everyone in Silicon Valley when he expanded from the
high-margin software business and entered the low-
margin hardware market by acquiring computer maker
Sun Microsystems for $7.4 billion.

Founded in 1982 by Bill Joy, Scott McNealy, Vinod
Khosla, and Andy Bechtolsheim, Sun Microsystems
created computer servers and workstations based on its
own SPARC (Scalable Processor Architecture) processors
as well Opteron processors (from Advanced Micro
Systems [AMD]) and Intel's Xeon processors. The firm also
developed and sold storage systems along with a suite of
software products including the Solaris operating system,
developer tools, Web infrastructure software, and identity

management applications. Other Sun technologies included the Java platform, *MySQL* (Structured Query Language), and NFS (Network File System). Sun was an active proponent of open systems in general and UNIX in particular, and a major contributor to the open source software movement. (Note: Open source denotes software for which the original source code is made freely available and may be redistributed with or without modification, thus encouraging collaboration, enhancement and the creation of new tools by third-party developers. Today, one of the prime competitors to the *Microsoft Office Suite* is the free *OpenOffice* collaboration suite. Meanwhile, the Free Software Foundation advocates aggressively for distributions and adoption of the free, open-source GNU/Linux.)

In many ways, Bill Joy provided much of the inspiration behind Sun's spirit of technical innovation. "There are geeks and then there's Bill Joy - 49-year-old software god, hero programmer, cofounder of Sun Microsystems and, until he quit in September, its chief scientist," wrote journalist Spencer Reiss in 2003. "Beginning in 1976, he spent zillions of hours in front of a keyboard, coding the now-ubiquitous Berkeley strain of the UNIX operating system; then he godfathered Sun's Java programming language and helped design servers that were the Internet's heaviest artillery. In the early 1990s, he kept his job but bolted Silicon Valley, 'leaving the urgent behind to get to the important,' he says."

In the spirit of *The Mythical Man-Month*, Joy to this day celebrates small systems design, small programming teams, and small implementations. "I've always said that all successful systems were small systems initially," he told Reiss in 2003. "Great, world-changing things - Java, for instance - always start small. The ideal project is one where people don't have meetings, they have lunch. The size of the team should be the size of the lunch table."

Joy's key mantra is innovation combined with leaps of faith. "If you look at the technology industry, you really have to believe in what you are doing and it needs to be great to make a difference," Joy commented in 2010. "The time to have been bold was when there was, perhaps, less reason to be bold, less apparent reason - right when Windows was cooking. If you remember back when Apple did the Mac, the Apple II was doing really well still. They had the Newton and it didn't work, so they haven't always succeeded, but they have been willing to be bold." (Newton was an early personal digital assistant and Apple's first tablet platform, which proved unpopular and was discontinued in 1998, in favor iOS, used in the iPhone.)

Today, as both a technical innovator and an investor associated with KPMG, Joy focuses his efforts on business plans related to green technologies, education and pandemic defense.

Finally, it is important to mention Cisco Systems. The firm was founded in 1984 by Len Bosack and Sandy Lerner (a couple who worked in computer operations at Stanford

University) and Richard Troiano. Cisco started out as a purveyor of communications routers, and quickly became the first firm to successfully sell commercial routers supporting multiple network protocols. As we shall see in a following chapter, with the eventual wide adoption of the Internet Protocol (IP), the need for multi-protocol routines concurrently declined. Thus today Cisco's most important routers are those used to deliver IP packets.

Cisco went public on the NASDAQ exchange in February of 1990 with a market capitalization of $224 million. In the midst of a shake-up seven months later, Lerner was fired and her husband resigned in protest. The couple walked away in disgust, but with $170 million, more than two thirds of which they eventually gave to charity.

Cisco continued to grow, largely through acquisitions. In the year 1995 - 1996 alone the company completed 11 acquisitions. Major firms that have over the years become part of the Cisco fold include Stratacom, Cerent Corporation and Linksys. A number of these acquired companies have grown into $1 billion+ product lines for Cisco, including major offerings in LAN switching, Enterprise Voice over Internet Protocol (VOIP), and home networking. At the height of the dot-com boom in March of 2000, Cisco briefly was the most highly-capitalized company on the planet, with a market capitalization of more than $500 billion.

There have been a few bumps in the road. In April of 2001, a class action lawsuit charged the firm with making

misleading statements in forward-looking financial
analyses that "were relied on by purchasers of Cisco stock."
Executives were also charged with insider trading. Cisco
denied all allegations, but in August of 2006 paid $91.75
million to bring the suit to an end. On another occasion, in
December of 2008, the Free Software Foundation (FSF)
filed suit concerning Cisco's failure to comply with the
GNU General Public License (GPL) and LGPL (Lesser
General Public License) and make the applicable source
code generally available. Cisco settled this lawsuit in the
spring of 2009 by complying with FSF licensing terms and
making a monetary contribution to the FSF.

Internet

"The Internet is becoming the town square for the global
village of tomorrow."
- Bill Gates, co-founder of Microsoft

Four decades ago, Vinton Cerf - widely known as one
of "the fathers of the Internet" and today VP and Chief
Internet Evangelist at Google - developed TCP/IP in
collaboration with Bob Kahn. TCP/IP, in turn, proved to be
the essential building block which enabled the creation of
the Internet.

According to Cerf, there were three critical phases in
the development of the Net. "The first was packet
switching," he comments, "which was independently
conceived by Leonard Kleinrock at MIT and UCLA,
Donald W. Davies at the U.K.'s National Physical
Laboratory and the late Paul Baran at the Rand
Corporation. Paul's work was in the early 1960s, when the
burning question was: How do you devise a voice and
data network that can survive a nuclear first strike?"

Cerf notes that the second phase was "actually
building a packet-switched network. The best-known one
was the Defense Department's ARPAnet, led by Larry
Roberts. Its purpose was radical: a network that could
share information across heterogeneous machines. Data

networks already existed in the 1960s, but these were networks of proprietary machines. SNA required IBM computers, DECnet required DEC computers, and so on."

The third phase, of course, was "building a network that could extend ARPAnet's machine independence by connecting to other networks. That's what Bob Kahn and I set out to do with the TCP/IP protocol. The Internet is literally a network of networks." TCP/IP stands for Transmission Control Protocol/Internet Protocol.

After Cerf and Kahn defined TCP/IP, Cerf as a program manager for the United States Department of Defense Advanced Research Projects Agency (DARPA) aggressively funded various institutions and research labs to develop TCP/IP technology. (Later on, during the late 1980s, as the Internet began to inch towards commercialization, Cerf moved to MCI where he played a key role in the development of the first consumer email system, MCI Mail.)

The Internet found its first function connecting research institutions and government agencies, and fostering communications between scientists and technologists worldwide. It was with these users in mind that Tim Berners-Lee launched a revolution.

Berners-Lee (British physicist, computer scientist and MIT professor) made the first proposal for what became the World Wide Web in March 1989. Less than one year later, on Christmas Day 1990 (with the assistance of Robert Cailliau, a young researcher at CERN [The European

Organization for Nuclear Research]) Berners-Lee
implemented the first successful Internet communication
between a Hypertext Transfer Protocol (HTTP) client and a
server. "Without Tim Berners-Lee and Robert Cailliau we
wouldn't have the World Wide Web," says Cerf, "without
which there'd be no avalanche of information flowing into
the Net. Information flow is what the Internet is about.
Information sharing is power. If don't share your ideas,
smart people can't do anything about them, and you'll
remain anonymous and powerless."

HTTP - via the language HTML (Hyper Text Markup
Language) - enabled easy navigation of the Net through
point and click movement across hyperlinks - thus
enabling one to seem to "surf" the information on the Web
from one related document to another. The first
significantly distributed and used client (aka, *browser*) for
the Web was *Mosaic*, developed at the National Center for
Supercomputing Applications (NCSA) at the University of
Illinois Urbana-Champaign beginning in late 1992 and
released non-commercially in 1993. *Mosaic* stands as
grandfather to all of today's popular browsers,
including *Netscape Navigator*, Mozilla's *FireFox*, *Microsoft
Internet Explorer*, Google's *Chrome*, and Apple's *Safari*.
Note: *Netscape Navigator* dominated browser market share
in the 1990s, but by 2002 claimed few users. *Navigator* lost
considerable market-share to Microsoft's *Internet
Explorer* because Netscape Communications Corporation
(eventually acquired by AOL) did not invest in the
development necessary to keep *Navigator* competitive. The
business demise of Netscape served as a central fact used

by the U.S. Justice Department in Microsoft's famous 1998 antitrust trial, wherein the Court ruled that Microsoft Corporation's bundling of *Explorer* with the Windows operating system constituted a monopolistic [and therefore illegal] business practice.)

At first, the idea of the Internet and the Web was highly idealistic: scientists and engineers and mathematicians at work on significant work, communicating in nearly real-time across the country and across the globe, and also publishing original research on a far more timely basis than was ever before possible. Others - in the spirit of the original small computer innovators and hackers - saw the Internet as a tool for breaking free from governmental control.

One of these was John Perry Barlow - former Wyoming cattle rancher, noted Grateful Dead lyricist, and earnest philosopher of all things digital. (Full disclosure: Barlow sits on the editorial board of New Street Communications, LLC, the publisher of this book.) In 1990, Barlow was the first to apply William Gibson's science fiction term "Cyberspace" to the global electronic social space now generally referred to by that name. Until his naming it, it had not been considered any sort of place.

In a seminal February 8, 1996 document entitled "A Declaration of the Independence of Cyberspace," Barlow posited the Internet as a new electronic frontier - a tribal no-man's land - a beautiful, flowering anarchy quite free from the strictures of government regulation.

"Governments of the Industrial World," Barlow wrote, "you weary giants of flesh and steel, I come from Cyberspace, the new home of Mind. On behalf of the future, I ask you of the past to leave us alone. You are not welcome among us. You have no sovereignty where we gather. We have no elected government, nor are we likely to have one, so I address you with no greater authority than that with which liberty itself always speaks. I declare the global social space we are building to be naturally independent of the tyrannies you seek to impose on us. You have no moral right to rule us nor do you possess any methods of enforcement we have true reason to fear. Governments derive their just powers from the consent of the governed. You have neither solicited nor received ours. We did not invite you. You do not know us, nor do you know our world. Cyberspace does not lie within your borders. Do not think that you can build it, as though it were a public construction project. You cannot. It is an act of nature and it grows itself through our collective actions. You have not engaged in our great and gathering conversation, nor did you create the wealth of our marketplaces. You do not know our culture, our ethics, or the unwritten codes that already provide our society more order than could be obtained by any of your impositions ... We are forming our own Social Contract. This governance will arise according to the conditions of our world, not yours. Our world is different. Cyberspace consists of transactions, relationships, and thought itself, arrayed like a standing wave in the web of our communications. Ours is a world that is both everywhere and nowhere, but it is not where bodies live. We are creating a world that all may enter without privilege or prejudice accorded by race, economic power, military force, or station of birth. We are creating a world where anyone, anywhere may express his or her beliefs, no matter how singular, without fear of being coerced into silence or conformity. Your legal concepts of property, expression, identity, movement, and context do not apply to us. They are all based on matter, and there is no matter here."

This philosophy was brilliant and idealistic - just like the bold vision of the revolutionaries at the old Home Brew Computing Club. But also like that lost dream for PCs, it was unrealistic. Barlow was, in fact, writing in the face of rising governmental regulations and looming commercialization: the settlement and development of the once lawless, and totally free, electronic frontier. Still, Barlow saw technical innovation as the domain of free and brilliant minds - these to be the inevitable, ultimate winners in a contest defined by new rules.

"In the United States," Barlow continued, "you have today created a law, the Telecommunications Reform Act, which repudiates your own Constitution and insults the dreams of Jefferson, Washington, Mill, Madison, DeToqueville, and Brandeis. These dreams must now be born anew in us. You are terrified of your own children, since they are natives in a world where you will always be immigrants. Because you fear them, you entrust your bureaucracies with the parental responsibilities you are too cowardly to confront yourselves. In our world, all the sentiments and expressions of humanity, from the debasing to the angelic, are parts of a seamless whole, the global conversation of bits. We cannot separate the air that chokes from the air upon which wings beat. In China, Germany, France, Russia, Singapore, Italy and the United States, you are trying to ward off the virus of liberty by erecting guard posts at the frontiers of Cyberspace. These may keep out the contagion for a small time, but they will not work in a world that will soon be blanketed in bit-bearing media."

In Barlow's view, the decentralized and pervasive nature of the Internet would itself put down all attempts at censorship and regulation. "Your increasingly obsolete information industries would perpetuate themselves by proposing laws, in America and elsewhere that claim to own speech itself throughout the world. These laws would declare ideas to be another industrial product, no more noble than pig iron. In our world, whatever the human mind may create can be reproduced and distributed infinitely at no cost. The global conveyance of thought no longer requires your factories to accomplish. These increasingly hostile and colonial measures place us in the same position as those previous lovers of freedom and self-determination who had to reject the authorities of distant, uninformed powers. We must declare our virtual selves immune to your sovereignty, even as we continue to consent to your rule over our bodies. We will spread ourselves across the Planet so that no one can arrest our thoughts. We will create a civilization of the Mind in

Cyberspace. May it be more humane and fair than the world your governments have made before."

Six years before, Barlow had co-founded the Electronic Frontier Foundation (EFF) with Mitch Kapor, former president of Lotus Development Corporation, and John Gilmore, an early employee of Sun Microsystems. The aim of these three men - who, by the way, first "met" each other in the digital space of the WELL - was to focus on civil liberties issues raised by new technologies. The organization has done so magnificently ever since. In large measure due to the diligence of the EFF, much of Barlow's vision for the Internet has remained intact - though certainly not all.

Many governments now control the ability to switch the Internet - or at least *much* of the Internet - on or off at will for the bulk of their citizenry. And laws in the United States and elsewhere continually nibble away at various Internet freedoms. In the pinch, however, technological innovation continues to trump bureaucracy, and probably always will.

"Look at how people have used online tools to advocate, organize, and recruit," comments Howard Rheingold. "Liverpool used to be the major port for England. Dock authorities offered a buyout package to close the port for commercial traffic. The dock workers went on strike, and used the web to mobilize other dock workers worldwide. Look at Radio station B92. The Serbian government shut down the radio station and everything went to the web. People are being able to use the medium effectively. Racists and Nazis do this too. Everyone gets the advantage. The tool does not automatically make something that is dull exciting. It extends our ability for people to continue to communicate, to organize, get the word out, diffuse information, to create a community network."

Note: Other key issues focused on by the EFF in recent years have included laws against the "export" of encryption technologies, and new threats not only to net neutrality but to free speech brought on by a host of commercial entities.

"While early threats to our right to communicate came from the government, current threats come also from industry, as it seeks to control and expand current revenue sources at the expense of traditional fair use," the EFF said in a recent statement. "The trend has been for industry to use a combination of law and technology to suppress the rights of people using technology. Nowhere is this more evident than in the world of copyright law, where the movie and recording studios are trying to dumb down technology to serve their 'bottom lines' and manipulate copyright laws to tip the delicate balance toward intellectual property ownership and away from the right to think and speak freely." The fight is ongoing.

Web Commerce

"The world is poised on the cusp of an economic and cultural shift as dramatic as that of the Industrial Revolution. (OK, it doesn't take a genius, or even a politician, to figure out that big changes are afoot when we have a medium that lets someone throw up a virtual storefront on the Web and instantly gain access to the global market.)"
- Steven Levy, journalist and author, 1997

What has become known as e-commerce - the marketing of goods via the Internet - began in 1991, when the Net was first opened to commercial use. Not until 1998, however, did e-commerce really begin to take off after the development of security protocols for HTTP. By 2000, the lion's share of large, "old-economy" businesses maintained web sites. At the same time, many "new-economy" "web-native" start-ups arose and - though for the most part they had yet to show a profit - quickly went public via IPOs fueled by wildly inflated expectations. This in turn led to the infamous dot-com collapse of 2000. In the aftermath, the firms with the worst and most unrealistic business plans died; but the ones with a real future hung on. By the end of 2001, the Business-to-Business (B2B) model of e-commerce (at that time the largest slice of the online economy) represented approx. $700 billion in annual transactions.

The first stars of the retail web included, and include, Amazon and eBay, the latter eventually encompassing the popular online payment system PAYPAL. These were quickly followed by such firms as Dell, Staples, Office Depot and Hewlett Packard. According to statistics, the most popular categories of products sold in the World Wide Web are music, books, computers, office supplies and consumer electronics.

Other firms have risen, and sometimes fallen, in providing search and related services on the Internet.

One of the first search endeavors was Lycos, developed in 1994 by Dr. Michael L. Mauldin and several other engineers at the Carnegie Mellon University Center for Machine Translation. (*Lycos* is the Latin name for the wolf spider.) Lycos started with a modest catalog of 54,000 web pages, but within a month its crawler software had "spidered" more than 390,000 documents, vastly expanding its index. Within a year Lycos had indexed 1.5 million documents, and it had accumulated data on over 60 million documents by the end of 1996 - vastly outpacing other search engines.

During June of 1995, Carnegie Mellon licensed Lycos to a new firm founded by Mauldin and backed by Carnegie Mellon in collaboration with CMG. The company went public the following year. In 1998 Lycos acquired Wired Digital, owner of the less-efficient HotBot search engine, and Mauldin left the firm. From this time on, Lycos developed as a portal network with many regional sites. The firm offered chat, personal home pages and additional features in an ads-driven model. Over time, Lycos' prominence as a search engine declined, this despite its 1999 decision to adopt the more-efficient FAST search technology.

One year later, at the most inflated moment of the dotcom bubble, Lycos was purchased for 12.5 million in stock by Terra Networks, S.A., a leading provider of Internet access to the Spanish and Portuguese-speaking world. Today Lycos remains somewhat viable in those markets, but takes its search results from Yahoo!

This latter firm also had university roots. According to Yahoo's official history: "The two founders of Yahoo!, David Filo and Jerry Yang, Ph.D. candidates in Electrical Engineering at Stanford University, started their guide in a campus trailer in February 1994 as a way to keep track of their personal interests on the Internet. Before long they were spending more time on their home-brewed lists of favorite links than on their doctoral dissertations. Eventually, Jerry and David's lists became too long and unwieldy, and they broke them out into categories. When the categories became too full, they developed subcategories ... and the core concept behind Yahoo! was born."

"Jerry and David's Guide to the World Wide Web" soon evolved into Yahoo!, this name an acronym for "Yet Another Hierarchical Officious Oracle."

Yahoo! celebrated its first million-hit day in the fall of 1994, this translating to almost 100 thousand unique visitors. Just a few months later, in early 1995, Filo and Yang formally launched their firm and received $2 million in venture capital from Sequoia Capital, the highly-respected Silicon Valley firm which had previously put money into such promising start-ups as Apple, Atari, Oracle and Cisco.

In due course, Filo and Yang hired Motorola management veteran Tim Koogle, an alumnus of the Stanford engineering department, as chief executive officer, and Jeffrey Mallett, founder of Novell's consumer division, as chief operating officer. Reuters Ltd. and Softbank provided a second round of funding in late '95, and the company (then boasting 49 employees) went public with a wildly successful IPO during early 1996.

Yahoo! grew rapidly throughout the 90s and, like Lycos, diversified into a Web portal. The firm's stock price shot to a high of $118.75 at the peak of the dot-com bubble, but afterwards reached an all-time low of $8.11. By 2008, in the face of stiff competition from Google and other players, Yahoo! was forced to enact several large layoffs.

During February of that year, Microsoft made an unsolicited bid to acquire Yahoo! for $44.6 billion. Yahoo! subsequently rejected the bid, claiming that it substantially undervalued Yahoo! and was not in the interest of its shareholders. Eleven months later, in January of 2009, Yahoo! appointed Carol Bartz, former executive chairperson AutoDesk, as its new chief executive officer and a member of the board. (Shortly, when asked on CNBC's Squawk Box whether she would have taken

Microsoft's initial bid of more than $40 billion, Bartz said: "Sure, do you think I'm stupid?") It is Google, however, which poses the largest problem for Yahoo! "Google is a fierce competitor," says Bartz. "I wish I was worth a bazillion dollars; that would be really nice. They're a fierce competitor and they're very good in search."

"Bartz has proven herself to be aggressive, foulmouthed, and utterly likable," comments journalist Cal Fussman. "But she still has to prove she can fix Yahoo! ... One of her first acts was to inform her staff that she would 'drop-kick to fucking Mars' anyone who leaked company secrets. Since then she's been trying to return Yahoo! to dominance, deliberately destroying everyone's impression of what it actually does. After a deal with Microsoft, Yahoo! is transforming from a search engine to a Web portal - one that, if Bartz is right, will attract new users (and new revenue) by trimming unwieldy Web searches down to personalized streams of information. She has her skeptics. But Bartz is right a lot, and most CEOs of her caliber don't earn their pay by luck. Neither do cocktail waitresses, and Bartz was once one of those, too. She knows when to give someone a 'bunny dip.' And she knows when someone needs a good drop-kicking."

"Tomorrow's Yahoo! is going to be really tailored," Bartz has said of her retooling of the troubled firm. "I'm not talking about organization - organizing means that you already know what you want and somebody's just putting it in shape for you. I'm talking about both smart science and people culling through masses of information on the fly and figuring out what people want to know. We will be delivering your interests to you. For instance, if you're a sports fan but have no interest in tennis, we won't show you tennis. We would know that you do things in a certain sequence, so we'd say, 'Here's your portfolio. Here's some news you might like. Oh, you went to this movie last week, here's some other movies you might want to check out.' I call it the Internet of One. I want it to be mine, and I don't want to work too hard to get what I need. In a way, I want it to be HAL. I want it to learn about me, to be me, and cull through the massive amount of information that's out there to find exactly what I want."

Of course, beyond Yahoo!, one of the most dominant success stories on the Internet is leading retailer Amazon (originally *Cadabra*, but then renamed by founder Jeff Bezos after the world's longest and most ecologically diverse river). Incorporated in 1994 and launched in 1995, the firm made its first annual profit in 2003. Amazon started out as an online bookstore but soon added electronics, software, DVDs, video games, music, apparel, footwear, health products and more. TIME named Bezos its 1999 Person of the Year in recognition of his central role in defining the new e-commerce marketplace.

Amazon's retail business extends to the United Kingdom, Canada, France, Germany, Japan, and China. As well, the company hosts and operates retail web sites for such firms as Marks & Spencer, Lacoste, the NBA, Bebe Stores and Target.

Amazon went public in 1997. "Silencing any doubts about its chances on the public market, Amazon ended the day $54 million richer as its long-awaited initial public offering soared 30 percent above its opening price," commented CNET on May 15 of that year. "Propelled by demand that pushed opening trading to 29-1/4, the pioneering online bookstore hit a day's high of 30 before settling down to close at 23-1/2. That was more than 30 percent higher than the $18 target price set by underwriters just the night before. Even that pre-IPO price had been raised twice before the market opened. Initially, it had been set for a $12-to-$14 range, then got bumped up to $14 to $16 before the company's investment bankers settled on the $18 price. The IPO raised $54 million for Amazon, giving the company a market value of $438 million. The online bookstore put 3 million shares on the block."

Today Amazon has further bolstered its business with the sale of eBooks and the popular Kindle eReader. Perhaps more importantly, it has also branched out into the high-growth area of providing cloud computing services via the Web for businesses large and small. Amazon has in fact become the market-leader in this space, where it competes head-to-head with such players as Google, VMware, Microsoft, Rackspace, Slaesforce.com, Joyent, IBM, NetSuite, and Tera.

Amazon enjoyed net sales of $34.20 billion in 2010, a 39.5% increase from $24.51 billion the previous year. And growth continues.

The elephant in the room of Internet commerce, however, is Google, begun as a search engine research project in 1996 by Larry Page and Sergey Brin, two PhD candidates at Stanford. Key to the new engine was a new search algorithm ("PageRank" technology) developed by the two to analyze relationships between websites - generating results determined by the number of pages, and the importance of those pages, that linked back to the original site. (Page and Brin at first referred to their new search engine as "BackRub," because of its checking of backlinks to gage the relevance of a particular web site. A similar strategy - "RankDex" - was explored at about this same time by Robin Li of IDD Information Services. Li subsequently used RankDex in founding the search site Baidu, in China.)

Eventually, Page and Brin changed the name of their enterprise to *Google* - derived from a chance misspelling of "googol" (the number "one" followed by one hundred zeros), this having been chosen because the word suggested a platform that would provide a nearly infinite quantity of categorized, high-quality information, thus maximizing the utility and value of that information. The two technologists turned entrepreneurs registered the *Google* domain name in September of 1997, but did not incorporate until September 1998. Since then, growth has been explosive, stemming from both in-house innovation and aggressive acquisitions. (In May of 2011, Google's unique visitors surpassed the 1 billion mark for the first time, an 8.4 percent increase from one year earlier and a *very* important fact since 99% of the Google's revenues

138

are derived from advertising via the firm's AdSense program and other products.)

Google received its first venture funding in August of 1998 - $100,000 from Sun Microsystems co-founder Andy Bechtolsheim. June of 1999 saw a second round of funding - $25 million from such venture firms Kleiner Perkins Caufield & Byers and Sequoia Capital. The IPO took place in August of 2004 - 19,605,052 shares (out of 272 million) offered at $85 per share. The IPO was handled via a revolutionary online auction system specially assembled by Morgan Stanley and Credit Suisse, who jointly underwrote the deal from which Google came away with a market capitalization of more than $23 billion. The vast majority of shares remained under the control of Google and its staff, most staffers becoming overnight millionaires. (Ironically Yahoo!, even though a competitor, made money as well, having provided support which resulted in its owning 8.4 million shares before the IPO.)

Google has branched out from search to providing productivity tools (such as Gmail), enterprise products, news delivery, eBooks, the open-source Android and Google Chrome operating systems, the open-source *Chrome* web browser, and cloud services. As of this writing the firm is preparing to launch *Google Wallet* for wireless payments from mobile devices.

For a good ten years early in the life of Google (2001 - 2011), Page and Brin acquiesced - largely due to demands from their venture funders - to seasoned manager Eric Schmidt as CEO. Under Schmidt - who ruled in something of a troika with Page and Brin, with Schmidt's being the most dominant voice - Google became the third largest tech company in the world - growing from less than $100 million in revenues to nearly $30 billion. As of 2011, Page has (amicably) reclaimed the CEO position.

"Page is *sui generis* and could potentially have the kind of impact Bill Gates and Steve Jobs have had," writes Steven Levy. "Nobody better encapsulates Google's ambitions, its ethics, and its worldview. At the same time, Page can be eccentric, arrogant, and secretive. ... Google's 2004 pre-IPO filing with the SEC included a note from Page to prospective shareholders. In it, he famously warned that 'Google is not a conventional company. We do not intend to become one.' In the ensuing years, Google made good on that promise. But under its ruling troika, Schmidt helped balance the founders' idiosyncratic urges with more traditional practices. With Page taking the helm, no one is sure how - or if - that delicate balance will be maintained. Now the company is in the hands of a true corporate radical."

The firm's corporate culture is informal and pleasant. Google's corporate philosophy advances such fundamental principles as making money "without doing evil," and that work should be both challenging and fun. To encourage out-of-the-box thinking, Google has invented a program called "Innovation Time Off" wherein engineers may spend up to 20% of their time on whatever might interest them, rather than on formal projects in development. This innovation program has led to some of Google's most profitable offerings, including Gmail, Google News, Orkut, and especially AdSense, from which so much of its earnings come.

However, Orkut actually represents a signal failure not of innovation, but of corporate vision. This social network was actually launched in 2004, well before the dawn of Facebook. "My dream was to connect all the Internet users so they can relate to each other," recalls Google engineer Orkut Buyukkookten as quoted in Steven Levy's *In the Plex*. The system allowed users to create profiles, join special interest groups, share photos, and so forth. The product proved quite popular with users, but Google did nothing to advance it. "The basic premise of social networking - that a personal recommendation from a friend was more valuable than all of human wisdom, as represented by Google Search - was viewed with horror by Google," Levy comments. "Page and Brin had started Google on the premise that the algorithm would provide the only answer." Orkut was therefore never a priority at Google, and was never improved - specifically by moving the processing to faster machines which would maintain performance as the user-base grew. "By the time Google switched Orkut's code base to a speedier infrastructure," writes Levy, "Facebook was beginning its rise." (Note: The remains or Orkut are included in Google's new social computing initiative, Google+, launched in July of 2011.)

"As Facebook and Twitter have shown," comments journalist Michael Rosenwald, "creating environments where humans control the information flow is a differentiating factor. Google has been forced to play catch-up with Facebook, whose audacious idea may be the most Googley of all. Google is responding by trying to socialize parts of the Web it already dominates, though *Buzz*, a status updater and photo sharer, hasn't caught on. Google's most recent response to Facebook's 'like' option allows user to assign '+1' symbols to search results they like - which also sounds gratuitously algorithmic."

The social aspect of online experience is generally referred to as Web 2.0. Here's a more formal definition: "The term 'Web 2.0' is associated with web applications that facilitate participatory information sharing, interoperability, user-centered design, and collaboration on the World Wide Web."

One of the first major enterprises in this area - after the start-up Friendster, which rose and fell with astonishing speed - was MySpace. This became the most popular social networking site in the United States in June 2006, a position that it held throughout 2007. But by April of 2008, MySpace found itself surpassed by Facebook when it came to unique monthly visitors. (As of May 2011, Quantcast estimated MySpace's monthly U.S. unique visitors at a mere 19.7 million.)

What went wrong?

Launched by Intermix in 2003, and enjoying nearly instant success, MySpace and its parent company were acquired by Rupert Murdoch's News Corp. in 2005 for

$580 million. "Mismanagement, a flawed merger, and countless strategic blunders have accelerated MySpace's fall from being one of the most popular websites on earth-one that promised to redefine music, politics, dating, and pop culture - to an afterthought," notes journalist Felix Gillette. "But MySpace's fate may not be an anomaly. It turns out that fast-moving technology, fickle user behavior, and swirling public perception are an extremely volatile mix. Add in the sense of arrogance that comes when hundreds of millions of people around the world are living on your platform, and social networks appear to be a very peculiar business - one in which companies might serially rise, fall, and disappear. ... In February 2009, with the threat of Facebook's growing popularity looming over their company, Chris DeWolfe and Tom Anderson, the co-founders of MySpace, appeared on The Charlie Rose Show. DeWolfe explained that MySpace was more than a social network; it was a portal where people discovered new friends and music and movies-it was practically where young people lived. 'We have the largest music catalog in the world,' DeWolfe said. Anderson predicted that by 2015, MySpace would have up to 400 million users. DeWolfe said the site's worth was 'in the billions.'"

But MySpace failed to meet competition with new innovation. Why? The founders blame the profitability demands of New Corp. A signal disadvantage, DeWolfe told Gillette, "was the pressure to monetize the site. While developers at Facebook, Tumblr, and Twitter-startups backed by venture capital-were more free to design their products without the immediate pressure of advertising goals, MySpace managers had to hit quarterly revenue targets. That pressure increased dramatically in the summer of 2006, when Google paid $300 million a year for three years to be the exclusive search-engine provider on MySpace on the condition that the social network hit a series of escalating traffic numbers."

DeWolfe: "When we did the Google deal, we basically doubled the ads on our site." Clutter ensued. And the blatant proliferation of ads became annoying for users.

Add to this the fact that while up-and-coming rival Facebook created an elegant open platform and wisely encouraged outside developers to build new apps, MySpace kept all software development in-house. "We tried to create every feature in the world and said, 'O.K., we can do it, why should we let a third party do it?'" comments DeWolfe. "We should have picked 5 to 10 key features that we totally focused on and let other people innovate on everything else." As of this writing, Rupert Murdoch - who not so long ago was delighted to acquire MySpace out from under the nose of another would-be purchaser, Viacom - is actively seeking a buyer for the troubled franchise, which he cannot get rid of fast enough. Viacom, meanwhile, is not interested.

Google's and MySpace's nemesis Facebook began to take root in October of 2003 when Harvard sophomore Mark Zuckerberg wrote *Facemash*, through which friends in the Harvard community could share ideas, photos, comments, and so forth. Just a few months later, when a promised official Harvard "facebook" network failed to materialize, Zuckerberg took matters into his own hands.

"When Mark E. Zuckerberg '06 grew impatient with the creation of an official universal Harvard facebook, he decided to take matters into his own hands," noted *The Harvard Crimson* on February 9, 2006. "After about a week of coding, Zuckerberg launched thefacebook.com last Wednesday afternoon. The website combines elements of a standard House face book with extensive profile features that allow students to search for others in their courses, social organizations and Houses. 'Everyone's been talking a lot about a universal face book within Harvard,' Zuckerberg said. 'I think it's kind of silly that it would take the University a couple of years to get around to it. I can do it better than they can, and I can do it in a week.' As of yesterday afternoon, Zuckerberg said over 650 students had registered use thefacebook.com. He said that he anticipated that 900 students would have joined the site by this morning. Zuckerberg's site allows people with Harvard e-mail addresses to upload their pictures and personal and academic information. Just as with the popular website Friendster, which Zuckerberg said was a model for his new website, members can search for people according to their interests and can create an online network of friends."

Within a month, more than half of all Harvard undergraduates had registered, at which point Zuckerberg and a small group of elves (Eduardo Saverin, Dustin Moskovitz, Andrew McCollum, and Chris Hughes) expanded Facebook to Stanford, Columbia, and Yale, and soon the majority of universities in North America. Next came high schools, then general interest users, then international expansion.

Facebook, which moved to Palo Alto, California in June, incorporated in the summer of 2004 with entrepreneur Sean Parker coming aboard as the company's president. One of the first major venture investors was PayPal co-founder Peter Thiel. Two years later, Microsoft purchased 1.6% of Facebook for $240 million, thus creating a $15 billion street-estimate of the firm's value. In 2009 Facebook aggressively pursued growth into foreign markets and became cash-positive. During November 2010 - according to the SecondMarket, Inc. exchange for privately-held shares - Facebook's value stood at about $41 billion: a figure eclipsing even that of auction site eBay. This made Facebook the third largest U.S. web company after Google and Amazon. As of January 2011, Facebook had more than 600 million active users around the world. Rumors suggest an IPO is likely in 2013.

As this book was being put to bed in the early summer of 2011, it was announced that one out of every ten people in the world was a Facebook user - a total of more than 750 million. "The social networking giant still has a lot on its plate," comments *TechCrunch*. "Current initiatives ... include creating a more accessible mobile platform, increasing the number of social games, and creating new ways to keep users informed on what their friends are up to. In addition to becoming one of the most powerful companies in the world, Facebook has itself become the launching pad for other companies. Success stories for Zynga, Foursquare, and other online start-ups were only made possible because of Zuckerberg and Facebook. The last time the social networking site officially commented on how many users it had was last summer (2010), when it announced it had reached the 500 million user milestone." Both Yahoo! and Viacom have at various times made acquisition offers - all rebuffed.

"Move fast and break things," Mark Zuckerberg (now, like Bill Gates, a Harvard dropout) famously tells his development team. "Unless you are breaking stuff, you are not moving fast enough." The philosophy works.

"Our whole theory," Zuckerberg has commented, "is that people have real connections in the world. People communicate most naturally and effectively with their friends and the people around them. What we figured is that if we could model what those connections were, [we could] provide that information to a set of applications through which people want to share information, photos or videos or events. But that only works if those relationships are real. That's a really big difference between Facebook and a lot of other sites. We're not thinking about ourselves as a community - we're not trying to build a community - we're not trying to make new connections."

Zuckerberg and his team clearly relish their project, their enterprise. "I was watching an interview with Steve Jobs the other day, in which he said that 'In order to be doing something like this, you have to really, really like what you're doing, because otherwise it just doesn't make sense.' The demands and the amount of work that it takes to put something like [Facebook] into place, it's just so much that if you weren't completely into what you were doing and you didn't think it was an important thing, then it would be irrational to spend that much time on it. Part of the reason why this is fun is because we've managed to build a team of really smart people who come from different backgrounds and have different experiences and think in different ways. People constantly try to put us in a bucket: are we trying to sell the company? What are we trying to do? What is the business strategy? People are often more interested in why we're hiring a stock-options administrator. Whereas for me and a lot of people around me, that's not really what we focus on. We're just focused on building things."

Other social networking and e-commerce successes? We know the names. LinkedIn. eTrade. Kayak. Expedia. And many, many more. Today we cannot imagine retail goods, travel-related services, information (including music and films) and financial services not being available via the Web. This is the measure of a revolution. Forrester Research predicts that total world online retail sales will total $250 billion by 2014.

The Future: Inter-Cloud, Etc.

"The best way to predict the future is to invent it."
                    - Alan Kay, computer scientist

The future is, in some respects, already here. Smartphones. Tablet computers. eReaders. And the Cloud. This latter item is the current hot area of innovation: the sharing of otherwise expensive computer capacity by diverse enterprises via the Internet in a "pay-as-you-go" utility model. The business of the cloud is ever expanding - in fact expanding exponentially. "... cloud computing is seeping into IT organizations and companies, often without any 'official' approval or strategy, but with the undeniable momentum of a locomotive," writes Bernard Golden, CEO of the consulting firm HyperStatus. " ... I firmly believe that we are on the cusp of more change in IT than we have seen throughout its history, and those of us working in the field have the enviable opportunity to be immersed in this transformation."

"I can only describe this now as a 'wow' moment," says Google's Eric Schmidt. "For me this is the beginning of the real revolution in information ... Fifty years ago people in America were getting very excited by the conversion from black and white television to color television. And computing was about building computers that had 1 megabyte, and that was the size of a small room ...

Doubling every 18 months is roughly a factor of 10 in five years. In 10 years that's a factor of 100. In 25 years it's roughly a factor of 100,000. So when you go back and you look at things 15 years or 10 years ago, understand that we were operating in the context of 1,000 times less computation, thinking, networking, data analysis - we just couldn't do it. We couldn't do the maps. We couldn't do the searches. We couldn't physically do it. You couldn't get enough hardware. You couldn't get enough power, whereas now it is trivial. So 50 years from now, people will think of us the way we think of the conversion from black and white to color television. They will think: 'Why couldn't they do these extraordinary things?'"

Schmidt continues: "When I grew up it was basically about enterprises - IT. Today computer science is really about consumers and information. The rise of Google, the rise of Facebook, the rise of Apple, I think are proof that there is a place for computer science as something that solves problems that people face every day. There was only one company that saw that a decade before anybody else and that company is Apple. If you look even through the nineties - Sun, Microsoft, Novell, Cisco - they were fundamentally infrastructure companies based around corporations. That is where the money was. There was almost no consumer use with the exception of Apple in people's daily lives. The big shift was over 10-15 years and it came with the development of the web. The easiest way to think about it is to imagine a non-technical person - a child, say. What is the first thing they would have done with technology? They would have used email. I noticed with my non-technical friends - their first foray into my world was the connection of the email system which occurred in 1991-1992. And then when the internet happened, the internet mail protocols became standardized, everyone else converted and you got this explosion."

Google evangelist and TCP/IP inventor Vinton Cerf, meanwhile, stresses the importance of something he calls the "Inter-Cloud." Cerf compares the current cloud situation to the lack of communication that hobbled individual computer networks pre-Internet. "At some point, it makes sense for somebody to say, 'I want to move my data from cloud A to cloud B,' but the different clouds do not know each other. We don't have any inter-cloud standards." Cerf visualizes multiple clouds interacting with each other in real time, forming on-demand banks of such combined processing power as has never before been known or imagined.

"People are going to want to move data around, they're going to want to ask clouds to do things for them," says Cerf. "There's a whole raft of research work still to be done and protocols to be designed and standards to be adopted that will allow people to manage assets."

Cerf also emphasizes the importance of security and - no surprise here - predicts a growing role for mobile devices in everyday life as well as the connections of more appliances, including home appliances and office equipment, via the Internet. "Once you do that, the mobile [device] is potentially the remote controller for all of these things," he says. "The mobile now replaces all those little remotes that are sitting on the table in front of you," says Cerf. In step with this prediction, and in recognition of the wireless capacity that will be needed, Cerf as well predicts the opening of access to "white spaces" - that unused broadcasting spectrum which today serves as a buffer between TV channels - as a tool for expanding broadcast access.

On another front, Cerf has "become very excited about optical switching as an efficient way of moving huge quantities of information back and forth." He further endorses the notion of IP-based television to support services such as on-demand programming. "A packaged-switch system can support on-demand more easily," he insists.

Futurist and inventor Ray Kurzweil notes that: "We're doubling the power of information technology every year, doubling the price performance, the capacity, the bandwidth, and it's not just electronics; it's really anything having to do with information, including, for example, biology ... It took us 15 years to sequence HIV; we sequenced SARS in 31 days. Our knowledge of the brain, which is our information processes, is doubling every year. The amount of data we have, the spatial resolution, our brain scanning is doubling every year. I mean, we could list 50 or 60 different information measures which are growing in this exponential fashion. Doubling every year means multiplying by a thousand in 10 years, a billion in 30 years - it's actually 25 years. If you think about how powerful - information technology - computers, communications, the Internet - our knowledge of biology is already, and then multiply that by a billion in 25 years, and the factor in the fact that it's also miniaturizing at a rate of five per linear dimension per decade, so these technologies in 3-D volume will be thousands of times smaller and a billion times more powerful, and you come up with some pretty remarkable capabilities."

Controversially and radically, Kurzweil looks forward to an eventual "singularity" between human and machine intelligence which will in effect lead to a sort of immortality. "We'll be able to capture human intelligence in a non-biological system - a machine, if you will - but these machines won't be like machines that we're used to. If you look at - and the hardware side of this equation is not even controversial; just look at Intel's Roadmap or the so-called ITRS Roadmap from the semiconductor industry, and you'll see that a chip in 2020 will have 5 nanometer features and will be as powerful as the human brain, a thousand times more powerful than the human brain by 2030. And the more important issues, the software, the methods of human intelligence, are being sort of unraveled through this grand project to reverse-engineer the human brain to understand its principles of operation. And there, again, we're making exponential gains in our understanding. We already have models, detailed mathematical models and simulations of a couple dozen regions out of the few hundred that exist in the human brain, and we can apply, for example, advanced psychoacoustic tests of this model of the auditory cortex and get similar results as applying these tests to human auditory perceptions. There's actually a simulation of the cerebellum where we do a skill formation, which comprises more than half the neurons in the brain."

The market ramifications of Kurzweil's theories remain to be seen.

On the more strictly and obviously commercial front, Apple has launched its revolutionary iCloud service for information consumers, directly competing with Google and Amazon for the sale and storage of music, film and other data in the cloud. Apple's iPad, meanwhile, leads the pack in the growing market for tablet computers, just as its iPhone reigns as the tech and market leader among smartphones. Innovation thrives at Cupertino under the close direction of the inimitable Jobs. At the same time, analysts and investors ponder what the firm will be like - and in what manner its innovation shall proceed - in an eventual post-Jobs world. Now shift focus over to Microsoft: an organization that seems mired in the past, focused on Windows and, after a host of failed product launches, stumbling in its attempts to innovate.

Elsewhere, everything that's old is new again. 2011 marks the 100th anniversary of IBM, and also the firm's first $100 billion year.

In the realm of books and newspapers, eReaders such as Amazon's Kindle and other digital publishing initiatives are actively redefining the nature and economics of publication - a revolution that has barely just begun.

Bottom line: Genius and invention flourish on a range of fronts and in a multitude of ambitious tech companies. Start-ups still start. Brilliant young men and women - impatient with the corporate culture of large organizations - still tinker-with and re-imagine the existing technology, intent on making it better, smarter, faster. New paradigms are devised and implemented. Myriad visions are pursued - some to bloom and dominate our tomorrows.

As it once did for Bill Gates, Steve Jobs and so many other pioneers, the future lies wide open - inviting us to invent it.

Editorial Note

Added July 24, 2012

This book was first published in a digital edition during July of 2011. Since then, we've had the departure of Carol Bartz at Yahoo, followed by the rise of Google wunderkind Marissa Mayer in her place. We've also seen the death of Steve Jobs (a reference to which I've in fact incorporated for this print edition), the Facebook IPO, and other events. But all books of written history must have a cut-off point. Especially in the computer field, where things change so rapidly. So, our cut-off date for the present volume is mid-2011. Perhaps in a few years I will do a revised second edition, extending coverage. But for now, this is where I'll leave it. Thanks much for reading, and I hope you enjoyed. - Lars Nielsen

About the Author

Lars Nielsen has more than thirty years experience as a systems developer and administrator for a range of *Fortune 500* companies. He lives in Amsterdam and is the author of New Street's bestselling *A Simple Introduction to Data Science,* as well as other works.

Also of Interest

Beast:
A Slightly Irreverent Tale About Cancer
(And Other Assorted Anecdotes)
By James Capuano
           "A surprisihgly life-affirming tale." - Susan Sarandon

Pete Seeger vs. The Un-Americans:
A Tale of the Blacklist
By Edward Renehan
           "Excellent, a truly enjoyable and informative read"
                                                    - Steve Buscemi

Hemingway's Paris: Our Paris?
By H.R. Stoneback
      "Stoneback's lyrical prose takes the reader inside the soul of
   Hemingway's Paris, penetrating the surface of guide-books to
                              reveal tantalizing secrets."
                                                    - A.E. Hotchner

Available in Kindle, Paper, and Audio Editions

newstreetcommunications.com